THE MAS. ⌐ ⌐ ⌐⌐⌐ SERIES

The Massey Lectures are co-sponsored by CBC Radio, House of Anansi Press, and Massey College in the University of Toronto. The series was created in honour of the Right Honourable Vincent Massey, former Governor General of Canada, and was inaugurated in 1961 to provide a forum on radio where major contemporary thinkers could address important issues of our time.

This book comprises the 2019 Massey Lectures, "Power Shift: The Longest Revolution," broadcast in November 2019 as part of CBC Radio's *Ideas* series. The producer of the series was Philip Coulter; the executive producer was Greg Kelly.

SALLY ARMSTRONG

SALLY ARMSTRONG is an award-winning author, journalist, and human rights activist. She is the author of four bestselling books: *Ascent of Women: A New Age Is Dawning for Every Mother's Daughter* (published in the U.S. as *Uprising: A New Age Is Dawning for Every Mother's Daughter*), *The Nine Lives of Charlotte Taylor*, *Veiled Threat: The Hidden Power of the Women of Afghanistan*, and *Bitter Roots, Tender Shoots: The Uncertain Fate of Afghanistan's Women*. Armstrong was the first journalist to bring the story of the women of Afghanistan to the world. She has also covered stories in conflict zones from Bosnia and Somalia to Rwanda and Afghanistan, Iraq, South Sudan, Jordan, and Israel. She is a four-time winner of the Amnesty International Canada media award, the recipient of ten honorary degrees, and an Officer of the Order of Canada. She was born and raised in Montreal, lives in Toronto, and spends the summer in New Brunswick.

Also by the Author

NONFICTION

Ascent of Women:
A New Age Is Dawning for Every Mother's Daughter
(published in the U.S. as
Uprising:
A New Age Is Dawning for Every Mother's Daughter)

Veiled Threat:
The Hidden Power of the Women of Afghanistan

Bitter Roots, Tender Shoots:
The Uncertain Fate of Afghanistan's Women

FICTION
The Nine Lives of Charlotte Taylor

POWER SHIFT

The Longest Revolution

SALLY ARMSTRONG

ANANSI

Published in Canada in 2019 and the USA in 2019 by House of Anansi Press Inc.
www.houseofanansi.com

23 22 21 20 19   1 2 3 4 5

Library and Archives Canada Cataloguing in Publication

Title: Power shift : the longest revolution / Sally Armstrong.
Names: Armstrong, Sally.
Series: Massey lectures series.
Description: Series statement: CBC Massey Lectures
Identifiers: Canadiana (print) 20189067829 | Canadiana (ebook) 20189067837
| ISBN 9781487006792 (softcover) | ISBN 9781487006808 (EPUB) |
ISBN 9781487006815 (Kindle)
Subjects: LCSH: Sex discrimination against women. | LCSH: Sex discrimination.
| LCSH: Women's   rights. | LCSH: Women—Legal status, laws, etc. |
LCSH: Women—Social conditions. | LCSH: Women— Economic conditions. |
LCSH: Social justice. | LCSH: Human rights.
Classification: LCC HQ1236 .A76 2019 | DDC 305.42—dc23

Cover design: Alysia Shewchuk
Cover illustration: Barry Blitt

*We acknowledge for their financial support of our publishing program the Canada
Council for the Arts, the Ontario Arts Council, and the Government of Canada.*

Printed and bound in Canada

For all the women and all the girls in all the world.
This is our time.

CONTENTS

Chapter 1: In the Beginning(s) 1

Chapter 2: The Mating Game 59

Chapter 3: A Holy Paradox 117

Chapter 4: When the Patriarchy Meets the Matriarchy 173

Chapter 5: Shifting Power 223

Notes 273
Permissions 299
Acknowledgements 301
Index 307

"I know that many men and even women are afraid and angry when women do speak, because in this barbaric society, when women speak truly they speak subversively — they can't help it: if you're underneath, if you're kept down, you break out, you subvert. We are volcanoes. When we women offer our experience as our truth, as human truth, all the maps change. There are new mountains.

That's what I want — to hear you erupting. You young Mount St. Helenses who don't know the power in you — I want to hear you."

— URSULA K. LE GUIN

CHAPTER ONE

IN THE BEGINNING(S)

SO MANY BEGINNINGS. From delicate handprints on a cave wall to goddesses in ancient Mesopotamia; from political tyranny that came in the guise of a message from God to the convoluted journey to emancipation — the story of women is the longest revolution in history. So many times change was in the wind. So many times the finish line blurred. And so many times hope soared. Still, from Toronto to Timbuktu, the promise of equality has eluded half the world's population. Now there's a power shift. There's never been a better time in human history to be a woman. And despite the blowback from misguided politicians, leftover chauvinists, and hypermasculine misogynists, women are closer to gaining equality than ever before. The journey ahead is bound to be epic, and it will affect everything — our wallets, our jobs, our very future.

Why now? How come the power shift didn't happen during the first wave of the women's movement (1848–1920), when the suffragettes struggled to get the vote? Or the second wave (1963–80), when women "put all our faith in the pill" and attended consciousness-raising sessions that discussed the oppression of women and demanded change in the status of women? Or even the third wave (1992–2010), which began after the American lawyer and academic Anita Hill was called to testify at the televised confirmation hearing of U.S. Supreme Court nominee Clarence Thomas, whom she had accused of sexual harassment, thus challenging his fitness for the position? Hill was then excoriated by the all-male Judiciary Committee, who didn't believe her, and Thomas was appointed to the Supreme Court. The fallout became a watershed moment in American politics and a turning point in raising awareness of sexual harassment. But still the long-term status of women was mostly unchanged.

Now with the fourth wave, a movement that began in 2012 when social media took off, there's a focus on intersectionality, a push for greater empowerment of traditionally marginalized groups — Indigenous people, people of colour; LGBTQ; ethnic, religious, and cultural minorities; people with physical and developmental disabilities; people of differing social classes — and for greater representation in politics and business. Fourth-wave feminists argue that society will be more equitable if policies and practices incorporate the perspectives of all people. While earlier feminists fought to shake off the ties that bound them to subservience, this new wave calls for justice against discrimination, assault, harassment, and it calls for equal pay and individual choices over our own bodies. Words like "cisgender," "non-binary," and "polyamorous" reflect the new vocabulary of a changing, more diverse society, and the clarion call for inclusion is being heard around the world.

This wave created hashtag feminism and put abusive powerful men on notice. And by all accounts, this one got liftoff. The symbiotic relationship between social media and individualism is likely driving the bus for change. The internet is all about "instant." Twitter and Facebook can elevate people and create extreme celebrity and propel movements. Some of these, like #MeToo and #TimesUp, have been amplified by attention from influential entities such as the *New York Times* and the Hollywood film industry, but others have been simmering over the last decade. As a journalist, I have watched human rights and the rights of women and girls become the focus of conversation, whether in the forests of the Democratic Republic of Congo or the savannah in Kenya, in the deserts of Afghanistan or the college campuses in North America.

We have always depended on political will to change up the agenda — the stroke of the politician's pen to install the stop sign or build the shelter or legislate a new law. It often took public will — marches and petitions — to push the politician to make change happen. But in the last few years, I'm seeing what I call personal will as the driving force behind both public and political will. Malala Yousafzai is a good example. She was fifteen years old, living in the Swat Valley in Pakistan; she wanted to go to school to learn to think for herself. But the Taliban, who claim they act in the name of God, forbade education for girls. She defied the cowardly thugs by speaking out publicly on girls' rights to an education. On October 8, 2012, she climbed onto the school bus. The last words she heard were: "Which one is Malala?" The Taliban gunman shot that child in the head for going to school. But Malala recovered, and then she started a movement. Today everyone knows her. She's become the world's daughter, not because a politician in the Swat Valley insisted that the girls go to school; not because there were marches and petitions demanding education for girls. It was personal will that propelled Malala.

The other telling side to this episode is that atrocities like this happen every day. But this time the world grabbed on to the story and didn't let it go. I believe it was more evidence of liftoff, of the changing status of women; proof that people realize that dismissing half the world's population is dangerous and expensive and wrong.

The holy grail for the social innovators of the twenty-first century is knowing how campaigns such as #MeToo and the rise in personal power can be sustained.

Jeremy Heimans and Henry Timms, authors of *New Power*, think they know the formula. They call it the difference between old power and new power. "Old power works *like a currency*," they say. "It is held by few. Once gained it is jealously guarded, and the powerful have a substantial store of it to spend. It is closed, inaccessible, and leader-driven. It downloads, and it captures."

As for new power, as exemplified by the #MeToo movement, it operates *"like a current. It is made by many. It is open, participatory, and peer-driven. It uploads, and it distributes. Like water or electricity, it's most forceful when it surges. The goal with new power is not to hoard it but to channel it."* Their conclusion is that #MeToo gave a sense of power to the participants, and that each individual story was strengthened by the surge of the much larger current.

Today that empowerment is taking on everything from date rape to old lingering mores that cling to the lives of women the way barnacles attach to ships, slowing them down, denying their fair passage. It is also fuelling change — enormous, life-altering change.

MY OWN VOYAGE on the equality caravan began with a kipper — a fish that's been split, salted, and dried — an unusual and ugly-looking concoction that appeared out of clouds of dense smoke puffing out of the boiling water in a large wrought-iron frying pan on Saturday mornings in my mother's kitchen. The kipper was served like food from the gods to my father, who sat at the end of the kitchen table. It was a ritual my Maritime mother executed for my Scottish father. My sisters and I watched, often wide-eyed, from our porridge bowls as this broad, flat, dark offering was picked apart and devoured with gusto. I thought the kipper breakfast was about Saturday mornings or being Scottish. Until I was eleven. That's when my baby brother, ten years my junior, was old enough to sit in a high chair at the kitchen table. And there, in front of my astonished eyes, my father was slipping tiny pieces of kipper to my brother. "There you are, laddie," he would say in his Highland brogue, with the pride of a patriarch. I had never been offered a piece of that frightful-looking fish. Nor had my sisters. Although I doubt we ever asked for a bite — nor had this small male in the high chair, who couldn't even talk.

It was the first time in my young life I realized boys got things that girls didn't. It wasn't about favouritism — my father was guilty of adoring all four kids. It was a ritual in the making — a father sharing his Scottish tradition with his beloved son, as his own father probably did with him.

I wasn't jealous, but I was perplexed. This moment marked the beginning of a long journey. It would be followed soon enough by more telltale signs that all was not equal between boys and girls. In high school, the girls' basketball team could only play two-thirds of the basketball court, while the boys played the full court. We could only dribble the ball three times — there was no such restriction for the boys. And when the weather turned nice and we went outdoors for track and field, the boys ran marathon races — the girls did not. In fact, women did not participate in the marathon at the Olympics until 1984 — almost ninety years after the men started competing in the 26.2-mile (42.195-kilometre) race. There were no team sports for women at the Olympics until 1964, when the IOC admitted women's volleyball because it was considered a non-contact sport.

Then, at university, the boys could carouse all night long, but the girls had curfews. While we did, no doubt, do our share of carousing, there was a powerful message underlying the systemic and societal codes of conduct that we absorbed as if by osmosis: "Women and girls are lesser, weaker, and not as valued as boys." Sports scholarships were for male athletes, not women athletes. And girls and young women who became pregnant disappeared — "gone to an aunt's," as author, journalist, and television host Anne Petrie described in her book about girls who were unwed, "in trouble," and ashamed. The father of the unborn child stayed on campus, strutting around like the cock of the walk. She was never seen in classes again.

Married women were bound by another set of baffling edicts. I was a child of the Sixties. Change was in the wind. We were knocking down old rules, old presumptions. But when it came to being, as Barbra Streisand sang, "Sadie, Sadie, married lady," dismantling the roles in a traditional heterosexual marriage was like trying to rewrite the holy texts. Women were expected to say "I obey" when they took their marriage vows. A married woman couldn't open a bank account without her husband's signature, couldn't seek hospital treatment for herself or her child without her husband's permission. Until 1969, birth control was illegal, while life-threatening abortions were still performed in back alleys. We had a lot to do — a long way to go.

Between 1957 and 1977, Doris Anderson, the first woman to be editor of Canada's best-known women's magazine, *Chatelaine*, turned the publication into the vanguard for the women's movement. Before Betty Friedan published *The Feminine Mystique* in 1963, Anderson was leading the charge with her sizzling magazine, raising issues no one dared to speak about before: incest, wife assault, child abuse. It would be decades before other realities, like date rape and workplace harassment, would make headlines, but Anderson was a pioneer in creating a safe public space for whispered conversations. Then, as now, the status quo was under assault. To many, the demands for change were unsettling and seen as an attack on decency and decorum. "You must hate being married if that's how you feel" was one common accusation. "Clearly you don't like being a mother" was another. It was also a time of miniskirts, high wet-look boots, and a fashion known as bra dresses. Hindsight brings a little comic relief — there we were, marching and demanding and accusing, seen as freedom fighters by some and as dames dressed like hookers by others.

It was a journalism assignment that made me decide to devote the rest of my career to the lives of women and girls, the obstacles they face, the sometimes horrifying consequences they suffer simply for being female, and the courageous steps they are taking to alter the status quo. In 1992, I was sent to Sarajevo to write about the effect of war on children. In the 1990s, the former Communist state of Yugoslavia imploded with a civil war that split the Balkans along ethnic and religious lines. The political upheaval and civil war led to the secession of Croatia, Serbia, Bosnia-Herzegovina, and Macedonia. The world looked on in horror as Sarajevo — the host of the 1984 Winter Olympics and home to Muslims, Serbs, and Croats — erupted into ethnic conflict: first the Muslim Bosnians and Croats against the Serbs, who wanted a Serb republic. When the Croats also turned against the Bosnians, the ugly term "ethnic cleansing" became a miserable fact in the lives of Muslims in Bosnia-Herzegovina, Croats in some pockets of Croatia, and Serbs in other parts of that country.

It was Sarajevo that made world headlines when it was under siege and the fighting turned into a bloodbath. The day before I was to leave that troubled city, I heard a rumour that Serbian soldiers were gang-raping the wives and sisters and daughters and mothers of Bosnians and Croatians. Journalists know well that often one of the first casualties of war is the truth. So my skepticism was running high. But as the day wore on, I kept hearing the story from credible sources. By nightfall, I was convinced there was some element of truth to the rumours. At the time, I was working for *Homemaker's*, the subversive little digest-size magazine that served up scrumptious recipes on one page and a blueprint to alter the status quo on the next. It would take about three months to get this story to press, so I diligently gathered up all that I could — names, mobile phone numbers, anecdotes, statistics — and when my plane landed in Canada, I gave my packet of data to an editor friend at a large news agency and said, "Give this to one of your reporters — it's a helluva story." Then I went back to my office to wait for the explosive headline.

I waited a week, another week, a third week. Nothing. Seven weeks later I saw a four-line report in *Newsweek* that read, essentially, "They are gang raping women in the Balkans." I called the man I'd given my data to and asked what had happened. He said he had been busy and had forgotten to assign the story. I was flabbergasted. Between twenty thousand and forty thousand women and girls were gang-raped, some of them as young as eight years old, some of them eighty years old.

At a staff meeting later that day, I expressed my dismay to the editors of *Homemaker's*. "Don't you get it?" they said. "No one wants the story — it's only about women." Everyone was in Sarajevo — BBC was there, so was CNN, the *Guardian*, the *New York Times*, CBC — some of the best journalists in the world were there, but not one of them covered the story. My editors said, "We should do the story." I replied, "It'll take us three months to get it to our readers." They said, "So — who else is doing it?" Soon enough, I was on a plane, going back to the region.

When the story was published, the facts went into the stratosphere: at last the news agencies picked up on the horrific truth of those rape camps. But there was still a protective silence around the details, partly because the women who had been raped were frightened that their families would find out and they would be rejected as damaged goods, and also because the Geneva Conventions, which outline rules of engagement and atrocities of war, made only one passing mention of rape. Many courageous women who survived the diabolical gang-raping in the Balkans went to the International Criminal Court in The Hague and had their case heard. In 1998, the Yugoslavia War Crimes Tribunal made rape and sexual enslavement in the time of war a crime against humanity. Only genocide is considered a more serious crime.

Our record is easily distorted. It took a women's magazine featuring recipes and fashion and beauty and decor to expose a war crime. The omission, diminishment, and erasure of women in the historical records has had serious implications for gender equality. Applying a gender lens to the many beginnings in women's lives — to the mating game, to customs and religion, and to politics and economics — will expose the flawed past and better inform the social transformation that is occurring today.

THE LATE GERDA LERNER, who has been hailed as the most influential figure in the development of women's and gender history, said, "Historical scholarship, up to the most recent past, has seen women as marginal to the making of civilization and as unessential to those pursuits defined as having historic significance." And that scholarship, up to the most recent past, has been dominated by men. As a result, most of what women have done historically has been left unrecorded, neglected, or ignored in the interpretation. And so the various beginnings created a blueprint for the lives of women in the last two millennia. The increasing number of women who have joined the fields of archaeology and anthropology has resulted in a re-examination of the past. When the lens changes focus, so do the facts.

Until the 1970s and '80s, those fields were dominated by men; an abundance of women researchers arrived only at the turn of the twenty-first century. That's why most of the collected data focused on what men were most interested in or the things that occurred to them. In traditional societies, they often had more access to male informants and male behaviour. So women's issues were not always apparent to them or shared with them, and by default they often downplayed women's roles in political, social, religious, and economic life.

Margaret Conkey, the first archaeologist to explore a gender perspective in the field, doesn't mince words when she talks about the past: women's prehistory is missing because only the male story was told. For example, the prevailing belief that men were hunters and women were gatherers, she says, has created a distorted view of the relationships between men and women that has influenced the way we interact with each other to this day. Simply put, she claims the research is permeated with assumptions, assertions, and statements of fact that are neither objective nor inclusive.

Words like "man" and "mankind" have always been presented as inclusive of all of humankind, when in fact they are exclusive terms that insinuate hierarchy and bias. What's more, our collective knowledge about ancient times portrays males as stronger, more aggressive, more dominant, more active, and in general more important than females. Females, in contrast, are presented as weak, passive, and dependent. And the research, which was done mostly by white, Western, middle-class men, focuses on issues that have a male bias: leadership, power, and warfare. The consequences are so far-reaching that it is fair to say today's status of women is a direct result of yesterday's interpretations.

Amanda Foreman, the British-American biographer and historian who wrote and hosted a four-part BBC series called *The Ascent of Woman*, says, "The hard truth is that in almost every civilization, women have been deemed the secondary sex. It's an idea that has become so ingrained it's been written into history as a biological truth." The financial and emotional cost of that truth is staggering. The worldwide cost of violence against women is a startling 2 percent of the GDP — that's $1.5 trillion, about the size of the entire economy of Canada.

Originally, archaeological and anthropological examinations of Stone Age *Homo erectus* and

Neanderthals (living between 3.6 million and ten thousand years ago) and of Upper Paleolithic Cro-Magnons (between fifty thousand and ten thousand years ago) rarely referred to women. We know they were there — sculptures of women with huge breasts, hips, and labia, found mostly in Europe but also in parts of Asia, have suggested goddess status for the reproducing woman. Recently — and I suspect this coincides precisely with the status of women becoming a focal point of the twenty-first century — both men and women experts in the field are re-examining the theories about the artifacts from prehistory and adding a new layer of knowledge — the gender layer.

In the 1970s and 1980s, Margaret Conkey, along with fellow American archaeologist Janet Spector and American anthropologist Ruth Tringham, pioneered the field of gender archaeology. They questioned researchers' assumptions, which were based primarily on some of the early ethnographies and the perception of gender roles. They pushed academics, as well as the public, to ask different questions in the research about the role of prehistoric women. Their goal was to make the invisible visible.

Now archaeologists and anthropologists suspect

there was a gender-neutral division of labour by the time *Homo sapiens* ruled the earth, starting three hundred thousand years ago. Archaeologist Dean Snow at Pennsylvania State University says that most of the handprints on the cave walls he studied in France and Spain were made by women, between twelve thousand and forty thousand years ago. A woman's index finger and ring finger tend to be the same length, whereas a man's ring finger is typically longer than his index finger. Snow discovered that despite the prevailing belief that the men were the artists, in fact three-quarters of the drawings were done by women. Why was it the women who did most of the cave art? Maybe because they were small enough to slip into the crevices, or maybe because they were the storytellers. Or maybe, as I would like to think, the artists wanted to leave their mark — a handprint to say, "I was here."

Studies of prehistoric tools used for baking bread and scraping hides have shown them to have fitted the hand of a female. Christopher Muscato, a historian at the University of Northern Colorado, says, "There was essentially no evidence to support the notion that men were the only ones making stone tools. There's also evidence that children may have been raised in a more communal fashion, with parenting being a group effort." This new gaze in the archaeological world casts a fresh lens on women, and on everything from initiation and birth to death rituals. Moreover, modern researchers are asking why anyone presumed a woman wasn't smart enough to make stone tools.

It's also been presumed that men, being larger in size and physically more powerful, would be the ones chasing down enormous mammoths and bringing home the bacon, so to speak, and that women, who had less physical power and were birthing the babies, would do more of the gathering, bringing home the berries, seeds, and nuts. Recent thinking by anthropologists and archaeologists suggests that, in fact, there wasn't a segregation of labour along gender lines, and all chores were shared between men and women depending on the needs of the group at the time.

Anthropologist Ian Hodder and his colleagues have studied a settlement dating back to 7400 BCE at Çatalhöyük, on the plains of central Turkey. They have so far uncovered eighteen different levels of settlement built one on top of the other over about 1,200 years — and proof of a time when women were equal to men.

"Thanks to modern scientific techniques, we

have seen that women and men were eating very similar foods, lived similar lives and worked in similar works," Hodder says. "The same social stature was given to both men and women. We have learned that men and women were equally approached." In fact, after birth the children were sent to live in other households in a kind of all-for-one, one-for-all society. Although men were taller and women were larger, there is "little indication that the sexes had specialized tasks or that daily life was highly gendered." Hodder's research showed "a high rate of infant and child mortality and several cases of burials of women with babies, perhaps indicating death during childbirth," but "no clear sign that any divergence in lifestyle . . . translated into differences of status or power." Almost everything he and his colleagues found, including death and burial rituals, suggests a society in which sex was relatively unimportant in assigning social roles.

However, Hodder says, one piece didn't fit: the art on the walls. The houses were filled with images of wild animals — bulls and stags with erect penises — and the very few paintings of females invariably depicted them gathering plants. But still, it was a society in which "the question of whether you were a man or a woman did not determine the life you could lead." He presumes the artwork was made to get in touch with the dead or protect them. He says that when you visit Çatalhöyük and go to these homes, and to the places where the dead were buried under the dwellings, "you can see both people and belongings of these people. It gives you the impression that your ancestors are still living with you."

Dr. April Nowell, chair of the anthropology department at the University of Victoria, says, "We can be confident in saying that both males and females were engaged in making art, tools, and even textiles. We can even say it may be that women were making the textiles as well as the nets for hunting. But that doesn't explain their status — at least not yet." She agrees that many of the clearly marked and delicately drawn handprints found in caves were made by women and maybe even girls, but to suggest those female artists were revered, exercised power, and had agency is a conclusion that cannot be drawn yet. In fact, she is concerned that the popularization of ancient female artifacts could lead to misinformation about women and that projecting our own ideas on the long-ago pre-civilized world could prevent us from seeing what was really there.

In a TEDx Talk amusingly titled "Paleo Porn," which she delivered in Victoria in November 2015, Nowell describes a 233,000-year-old figure found in Israel. She admits it was hard to know at first whether this was a sculpture of a woman or just a strangely shaped rock. Others suggested it might be a penis or a penguin. After much analysis, researchers agreed the figure was of a woman and that it was carved with stone tools. In her lecture, Dr. Nowell further examines our views of these figurines and how those views reflect our own thinking on the status of women. She refers to the headless engraved Aurignacian "Venus" of Hohle Fels, dating to 35,000 BCE, which created a sensation when it was discovered in a cave near Schelklingen, Germany, in 2008. Its dimensions (six centimetres in length) are modest, but its morphology inspired hyperbolic introductions in the mass media.

Nowell showed the audience an article from *Discovery Magazine* that referred to the figurine as having "prodigious hips and mammaries — and titanic labia." (The article described another prehistoric figurine as having "GG-cup breasts and a hippopotomal butt.") She kept copies of the headlines that variously described the Venus figurine as the "world's first Page 3 Girl" (*Sun*, 2009) and "smut carved from a mammoth tusk" (*Economist*, 2009). Even scientific publications weighed in with sexist remarks. The academic journal *Nature* referred to the figurine as a "prehistoric pinup" and a "35,000-year-old sex object," while *Science* magazine asked whether the figurine could be the "earliest pornography." To her horror, the Urgeschichtliches Museum Blaubeuren, where the Hohle Fels figurine is housed, advertised it as an "earth mother or pin-up girl." In an article headlined "Archaeologists Unearth Oldest Known 3D Pornography," the *Register* newspaper quoted a well-respected Paleolithic archaeologist, who stated the figurine is "sexually exaggerated to the point of being pornographic" and that "there's all this sexual symbolism bubbling up in that period. They were sex-mad."

Dr. Nowell, a charming, energetic scientist who shares her findings with the relish of a storyteller, feels this kind of rhetoric about artifacts being sexual objects reduces the value of the research as well as the status of women. The study of women is often based not on what we see but on who sees it, and when. The Kinsey Reports on human sexual behaviour, *Sexual Behavior in the Human Male*

(1948) and *Sexual Behavior in the Human Female* (1953), found that women were less likely than men to be aroused by nude photos of the opposite sex. But, Nowell says, "If you flash forward in time to the present day . . . one in every three visitors to adult sites are women, and studies . . . show that in fact woman are aroused by visual stimuli." She attributes this shift to "historical changes . . . the rise of feminism, the availability of the birth control pill, and changes in our attitude towards sex more broadly."

When the Duke and Duchess of Cambridge (Kate Middleton and Prince William) went to the Solomon Islands, they were presented with flowers by bare-breasted women. But at precisely the same time, the couple was suing a French magazine for publishing photographs of Middleton sunbathing topless. "Whether bare breasts are taboo or not depends on who you are and where you are," Nowell says. "If we take a figurine . . . and all we see is pornography, what does that say about us and how we see women?" If instead we see a chance to better understand our ancestors, she concludes, it may tell us a little more about who we are today.

I asked Nowell what she thought about the

switch in emphasis around women. "I would say more women in the field of anthropology (cultural anthropology, archaeology, and biological anthropology), and the rise of feminism more broadly, led to more of an emphasis on researching women (and even children) in the past. Women may be in the collective conscious now, but this change in focus has a longer history in archaeology," she said. "Even as more women entered the field, there was still some bias inherent in the system — there was a study done showing that women more often received grants for archaeological lab work ('housework') than for archaeological excavation."

Throughout history, women have been subject to this sort of reductionism. The ever-enduring notion of the virgin versus the whore leaves no room for the complexity that better explains human nature. As for discovering whether women had agency and power in paleolithic times, the researchers are still at work. My bet is they did.

THE ERA THAT FOLLOWED the Stone Age is known as the agriculture era. It ushered in farming and the domestication of animals about ten thousand years ago. For the first time, there was a surplus of food and therefore the luxury of planning for the future, albeit a future that meant growing and storing enough food to survive to the next planting season. There's nothing quite like a bumper crop to boost morale as well as the health of the family. That's precisely what happened when seeds found their way into rows of cultivated farmland. And surplus seemed to be the ticket to currency (trade you my basket of tomatoes for your fine pig) and power (this is my land). Hunting and gathering were replaced by individual ownership of land and the building of houses. The woman was the guardian of the domestic fire; she invented clay and woven vessels for saving surplus food. She's the one who figured out that there were healing properties in some plants, trees, and fruits. She turned raw materials into hemp, yarn, and clothing. She played as much of a role as men did in the development of rituals, rites, music, dance, and poetry.

But this is also when women's sexual reproductive capacity was appropriated by men in order to produce more labourers. Pregnant women were acquired by men; so was land, which was being privatized for the first time. This combination marked the birth of patriarchy.

The first form of civilization had in fact begun

earlier, in 12,000 BCE, with the evolution of seden-
tary (as opposed to earlier nomadic) cultures. It's the
Sumerians, who lived in Southern Mesopotamia
(present-day Iraq), who can claim bragging rights
for the birth of civilization. They led the pack in
development — first irrigation, then the wheel in
3500 BCE, then the plough and writing around
3000 BCE. During that time, women thrived. They
bought their own property and could get divorced.
A woman had the right to control her own inheritance, open her own business, and lead her own
life, without the permission or control of her husband, brother, or son — or any other man.

The bright shining star of the era was
Enheduanna, daughter of Sargon of Akkad, known
as a great empire builder. Born in 2285 BCE, she lived
in the Sumerian city-state of Ur. She was elevated to
high priestess, and her job was to create stability in
the empire. She was the first named author in world
history. She was the first woman to identify herself
by signing her name to her work, as she did to many
of her poems, perhaps declaring to the world, "I AM,"
much as the Stone Age cave artists left their handprints on the cave walls to say, "I was here."

But the sands of power were shifting, and the
Sumerians were being absorbed, first in 2334 BCE by

the Akkadians, who created the world's first empire of Mesopotamia, and soon after by the Assyrians. The first Assyrian cities were Mosul, which the world came to know during the ISIS uprising, and Nineveh, which is still referred to as the Iraqi province of "the original people" — the Assyrians (the ancestors of the Assyrian Christians) and the Yazidis occupied this land for centuries.

After Enheduanna died in 2250 BCE, the Assyrians took control of the entire region. That's when legalized patriarchy became more entrenched.

The 112 Assyrian laws are housed in the national museum in Berlin, Germany. They include the first veiling law for women, two thousand years before Islam. More than half the laws deal with marriage and sex. Women were divided into five groups: wives and daughters of the upper class, concubines, temple prostitutes, harlots, and slave girls. The laws are powerful evidence of the double standard women lived with — a man could abuse his wife up to but not including the point of killing her. And punishments were brutal: a slave girl caught wearing a veil (the garment of an upper-class woman) would have her ears cut off, and women who committed adultery or had abortions were executed.

Patriarchy, it seems, is obsessed with women and sex and marriage. The scholar Cynthia Enloe says, "Patriarchy is built on sexism, misogyny, gender inequality. It's authoritarian and perpetuates domination, intimidation, and subordination."

While patriarchy seems to have been born and nurtured during the beginning of the agricultural era, it was most certainly perfected when religion became a formalized affair and was codified as laws, such as Assyrian laws and the codes of Hammurabi — the Babylonian laws governing modern-day Iraq from 1792 to 1750 BCE, including the first eye-for-an-eye and tooth-for-a-tooth laws.

Even today, laws codify patriarchy. Witness a recent contribution to the debate about women's right to drive in Saudi Arabia. Women have been allowed to drive there only since 2018, and while that seems ludicrous in the twenty-first century, it was Kamal Subhi, an academic, who went to the legislative assembly in 2011 and explained that allowing women to drive a car would spell the "end of virginity" in the kingdom. Really? Then I heard him on the CBC: I was driving my car, and my friend Maggie was sitting in the front seat with me. We heard him say, "What people don't understand is when a woman drives a car, she stops ovulating." "Gee, I wish I'd known that," Maggie said drily.

But I am ahead of myself. Let's get back to the Greek and Roman Empires and see how the women were faring. The organization of society along patriarchal lines reinforced by belief systems can really be seen in ancient Greece and Rome. While the oppression had already been established with religious doctrines and codified laws, the writings and orations of the Greek and Roman era reinforced a bias against women and, for the most part, supported their exclusion. The rights of women would rise and fall depending on the whims of rulers, but chauvinism was always the order of the day. And this was reflected in the teachings that scholars provided and that students have absorbed ever since. Names from these eras are entrenched in our schooling: Greeks like Homer, Socrates, Plato, and Aristotle; Romans like Julius Caesar, Mark Antony, and Augustus. The Greeks gave us philosophy, mathematics, astronomy, medicine, and architecture, while the Romans invented the calendar we use today and concrete structures like aqueducts and heating systems. Ancient Greek women were secluded and denied citizenship, could own but not sell property, and were subject to their fathers all of their lives. Roman women were subject to either their fathers or their husbands, but because they had citizenship, they could own and sell property and go about their lives mostly as they wished. By 300 BCE, the two leading cities in Greece, Athens and Sparta, had completely different laws and social codes for women. Athenian women had no rights whatsoever: they couldn't own property, they stayed at home, they were not taught to read and write, and they married young — about age four-teen — in arranged marriages, usually to an older man. In Sparta, women were expected to help defend the city; they were educated, played sports, married later and by choice, owned land and prop-erty, and even debated with men.

Although a woman had the right to own prop-erty in Rome, it didn't translate to emancipation; she was still under guardianship and was expected to be silent and invisible in intellectual and polit-ical life. Even though the Roman Empire devoted considerable energy to developing natural law and the rights of citizens, a Roman woman remained without political and legal rights.

Women's rights were not top of mind even for intellectuals like Plato, Aristotle, and Cicero. Although this period produced some of the most lauded writers and philosophers in history, and still today we read their writing (such as Aristotle's *Politics* and Cicero's *On the Laws*), it includes patriarchal and misogynist ideas that reinforced the lower status of women during that time and that have been perpetuated over millennia.

Just as in today's version of the debate, religious leaders relied on the holy scriptures for their arguments, while scholars claimed that the concept of human rights was secular. In either case, women's voices were generally excluded during the rise and fall of both empires.

Across the water in Egypt, women were taking back their rights by 69 BCE and moving into a political role. Author and historical biographer Stacy Schiff details the lives of Egyptian women in her biography of Cleopatra. She describes how a woman had the right to choose her own husband, to inherit, to hold property, to divorce. Women lent money and operated barges, served as priests, initiated lawsuits, hired flute players, and owned vineyards. Schiff writes, "As much as one third of Ptolemaic Egypt may have been in female hands."

In the East, Confucian theories took hold in China, Korea, Japan, and Vietnam for more than two millennia. Developed as a system of social and ethical philosophy between the sixth and fifth centuries BCE, Confucianism still influences styles of governance, education, and family for many Chinese. Dating back to about 1000 BCE, China had been a matriarchal society with the differentiation of male (yang) and female (yin) principles. "It was Confucianism that turned the marriage system into bondage of women, treating them as possessions for their husbands," the scholar Xiongya Gao says. "As the most influential school of thought in China, Confucianism was held as the dominant social ideology by almost every feudal dynasty from 200 BCE to 1911, when the Qing Dynasty was toppled, and by the nationalist government, which ruled the country from 1912 to 1949."

Women were expected to observe the Three Obediences: obedience to the father and elder brothers when young; to the husband when married; and to the sons when widowed. And the Four Virtues: propriety in behaviour, speech, demeanour, and employment.

Other Confucian rules include:

- A woman's duty is not to control or take charge.
- Woman's greatest duty is to produce a son.

- A woman ruler is like a hen crowing.
- The woman with no talent is the one who has merit.
- Disorder is not sent down by Heaven; it is produced by women.
- Women are to be led and to follow others.
- A woman should look on her husband as if he were Heaven itself, and never weary of thinking how she may yield to him.

Japanese women didn't fare a lot better. Japan imported Confucianism in the sixth century CE, with its underlying principles of humanity, loyalty, and morality. Women could converse with men only from behind a curtain. They wore layers of clothes that completely obscured the female form. Female beauty was important but was judged by the artistry of a woman's calligraphy and the colours and layers of her clothes. Japanese women didn't emerge from these stultifying rules until the 1930s, although patriarchal hierarchy still informs life in these societies.

DESPITE THE KINGS and philosophers and holy men who dismissed women as "hens crowing" and worse, the struggle by women (and some men) to advocate their status as equals never stopped. The current struggle to establish equality began in 1405, during the late Middle Ages, when the French-Italian author Christine de Pizan published a novel called *Le Livre de la cité des dames*. Pizan has been hailed as the first female author to make her living by writing. In the novel, she constructs three allegorical foremothers: Reason, Justice, and Rectitude. Together they create a dialogue that addresses issues of consequence to all women: a woman's right to education; her right to live and work independently; and her right to participate in public life and take responsibility for herself. After her death, her books continued to be popular, and her book *Faytes of Arms* was one of the first published with the printing press started by William Caxton in England. Henry VII asked Caxton to print a special English edition so that his knights could be up to date on military technology — but Christine's name was left off the cover because it was believed that the knights would not accept a woman's advice on military matters.

The fifteenth century brought witch trials, whereby those who were accused of worshipping Satan were burned at the stake. Over 75 percent of the victims were women, often targeted for nothing more than their outspokenness or their religious beliefs. Women were generally seen and not heard, expected to mind the hearth and perfect their needlework. But there were many exceptions. In 1513, Henry VIII left England to fight in France and appointed his queen, Catherine of Aragon, governor of the realm and captain general of the home forces in his absence.

In most cases, marriages were arranged, divorce was unknown, and legally a girl could marry at the age of twelve. Education for girls was not generally available, although girls from wealthy families were educated at home, and some upper-class women were very highly educated. Queen Elizabeth I was also educated and was apparently an avid reader.

The late seventeenth and eighteenth centuries saw the rise of the Enlightenment period, also known as the Age of Reason. Scholars thought they could uphold reason and intellect over God and religion. They referred back to the Middle Ages, the fifth to the fifteenth centuries, as the "Dark Ages."

Thomas Hobbes was one of the first Western philosophers to claim equal status for women. In his assertion of the equality of all people, he explicitly included women; his social contract among persons counted women as persons. He insisted that women and men are "naturally free" to an equal extent. But as much as Hobbes spoke and wrote of egalitarianism, he used the language of patriarchy. Families were referenced as fathers, servants, and children. He claimed that fathers, not mothers, founded societies. That contradiction is perhaps why he remains an enigma.

His colleagues didn't agree with his views about women. Although women were attending salons, coffee houses, debating clubs, and academic competitions, and were writing their own theories, male political thinkers such John Locke, Jean-Jacques Rousseau, Immanuel Kant, and Robespierre asserted the human right to defy religious authority but they did not champion the cause of women. In fact, even though Rousseau had conversed with highly intelligent women in the salons, his writings were misogynistic. In his book *Emile, or On Education*, he wrote, "Men and women are not equal; it is the part of one to be active and strong, the other to be passive and weak. Woman is intended to please man and their education must be wholly directed to give them pleasure, and to be useful to them."

Then, as now, it was left to women to insist that they be included in the discussion of human rights. In 1791, the French playwright and activist Olympe de Gouges published *Déclaration des droits de la femme et de la citoyenne*, demanding that French women be given the same rights as French men, including the right to bodily integrity and the rights to vote, to hold public office, to work, to fair or equal pay, to education, to own property, to serve in the military, to enter into legal contracts, and marital, religious, and parental rights. She famously said, "A woman has the right to mount the scaffold. She must possess equally the right to mount the speaker's platform." She dedicated the work to Queen Marie Antoinette, hoping that a member of the royal entourage in France would support the causes of women. After the overthrow of the monarchy, she was suspected of harbouring royalist sympathies. In 1793, Gouges was accused of sedition, arrested, and beheaded.

A year after Gouges's *Déclaration* came *A Vindication of the Rights of Woman*, by the English women's rights advocate Mary Wollstonecraft, who claimed that women are human beings, not ornaments or possessions, and are entitled to the same fundamental rights as men. Her husband, the novelist and philosopher William Godwin, campaigned for women's rights, and so did the poet Percy Bysshe Shelley, who married their daughter Mary, the author of *Frankenstein*. While Wollstonecraft called for equality, she stopped short of saying that women are equal to men. That's why some modern feminists claim she wasn't feminist enough. Wollstonecraft did say women had the same ability to reason as men, but she warned women not to be overly influenced by feelings.

During the nineteenth-century industrial age, the concept of socialism entered the lexicon of common language. Micheline Ishay, the author of *The Human Rights Reader*, lists the emancipation of women, along with the prohibition of child labour and the establishment of factory health and safety measures and universal voting rights, including a woman's right to vote, as major advances promoted in the writings of Karl Marx.

John Stuart Mill championed equality between the sexes in the British parliament when he called for suffrage in 1867. He said marriage — which deprived a wife of property and legal personhood, and forced total obedience to her husband — was akin to slavery. Coverture was a legal doctrine in the U.K. that declared that a wife's rights were subsumed in those of her husband: a husband and wife were one person under the law, and that person was the husband. Until 1870, a married woman was not allowed to pursue an education without her husband's consent, possess her own property, or sign or enter into a legal contract. If she was allowed to work, her husband was entitled to her wages. In some cases, a woman could be spared legal liability for her actions on the basis that her husband must have directed them.

Given the accepted beliefs of the time, Mill made an enormously daring suggestion when he stood in the House of Commons in 1867 and tried to change the wording of the Representation of the People Act from "men" to "persons." As Jamie Bartlett writes in *Radicals Chasing Utopia,* Mill's proposal "sparked a furious and mocking response. English masculinity would be threatened, said opponents. His proposed amendment would debase women. Mill was roundly defeated. 'Mr. Mill might import a little more common sense into his arguments,' said one member of parliament at the time."

In his 1869 essay *The Subjection of Women,* Mill wrote, "We are continually told that civilization and Christianity have restored to woman her just rights. Meanwhile, the wife is the actual bond-servant of her husband: no less so, as far as the legal obligation goes, than slaves."

The dawn of the twentieth century saw the rise of the first wave of feminism. The suffragettes picked up the torch for equality and the right to vote in Britain in 1903, when Emmeline Pankhurst, the British political activist whose motto was "deeds not words," founded the British Women's Social and Political Union. The union used militant tactics to agitate for women's suffrage. They heckled, stormed, battled, and accused their opponents of denying rights to women; finally, in 1918, women over the age of thirty won the right to vote. Pankhurst was imprisoned many times for her efforts. Her militant tactics drew widespread criticism, and some historians question their effectiveness. But in 1999, *Time Magazine* named her one of the 100 Most Important People of the 20th Century, stating, "She shaped an idea of women for our time; she shook society into a new pattern from which there could be no going back."

New Zealand had already granted women from the age of twenty-one the right to vote, in 1893. Britain clung onto its restriction for ten years, and then in 1928 the law changed and women aged twenty-one and older could vote. In the U.S., the

Nineteenth Amendment, which granted women the right to vote, was added to the Constitution in 1920. In Canada, Manitoba was the first province to give women the right to vote, in 1916, followed soon after by Saskatchewan and Alberta. By 1922, all provinces except Quebec were on board. Quebec women won suffrage in 1940. Until 1960, First Nations people could not vote in an election without giving up treaty rights.

And there was another battle brewing in those early suffrage days. In 1928, the Supreme Court of Canada ruled that women, because they were not considered persons under the law, were ineligible to be named senators. Five women from Alberta — Emily Murphy, Nellie McClung, Louise C. McKinney, Henrietta Muir Edwards, and Irene Parlby — took on the case and appealed to the Privy Council. On October 18, 1929, the British Judicial Committee of the Privy Council overturned the Supreme Court ruling. The victory came to be known as the Persons Case, which is celebrated in Canada even today, and the women came to be known as the Famous Five.

In 1902, international government delegates at The Hague, prompted by pressure from the women's suffrage movement, adopted a series of conventions, including the Hague Guardianship

Convention, to establish international standards for marriage, divorce, and child custody. It marked the beginning of a century of change for women.

At the 1919 Paris Peace Conference after the First World War, the Allied powers drafted the Covenant of the League of Nations, which included legislation supporting "fair and humane conditions of labour for men, women, and children." The catastrophe of the Second World War spurred the Allies and other nations to establish an international institution to prevent global conflict. On April 25, 1945, they met in San Francisco and began drafting the Charter of the United Nations. The UN Economic and Social Council established the Commission on Human Rights in 1946; in an effort to avoid any recurrence of the wartime atrocities, it drafted a document outlining individual rights.

The language of the Charter was controversial in terms of gender. Eleanor Roosevelt resisted changing the term "all men" to "all people" or "all human beings"; to her, "all men" meant "all people." The UN Commission on the Status of Women advocated for changes but was rebuffed. The committee, after extensive deliberation, settled on "all people, men and women," but the phrase "all human beings" ended up in the final report, reportedly because of a hitch in the drafting process. Despite all these efforts, the terms "mankind" and "he" remained in some passages.

On December 10, 1948, the United Nations General Assembly adopted the Universal Declaration of Human Rights. It asserted that all people are equal "without distinction of any kind such as race, colour, sex, language . . . or other status." For the first time, sex equality was enshrined in an international agreement as a fundamental human right.

However useful the Charter may be — along with the declarations, covenants, and conventions that have followed — the UN lacks the power to enforce. The documents depend on the goodwill of signatory governments. As such, they are primarily effective in the politics of embarrassment.

With the 1960s came feminism's second wave. Women such as Betty Friedan and Doris Anderson called for legal rights, workplace rights, and equality in the home, in the bedroom, and on the street. Those were heady days for women who fought to alter the status of women, and there was a level of excitement fuelling the debate. In 1972, Helen Reddy's "I am woman, hear me roar" resounded like a call to arms. But somehow it wasn't enough.

The backlash from many men and some women, who accused feminists of everything from hating men to being bad mothers and wives, reminded women that patriarchy touches every aspect of our lives. There's no doubting the gains women made in those exhilarating days — to open a bank account in her own name, to run a marathon, to become an astronaut. But they didn't establish equal pay or get her a job in the C-suite, or stop the violence, or bring a halt to sexual assault.

This is the torch women have carried ever since. And it's burning ever brighter now: In 2014, Malala Yousafzai won the Nobel Peace Prize for having defied the Taliban, survived their murderous attack, and gone on to start a movement promoting education for girls. In 2006, Tarana Burke started using the phrase "Me Too" to promote empowerment among women of colour who had experienced sexual abuse. In 2017, #MeToo turned into a mass movement protesting workplace sexual harassment assault. #TimesUp followed on January 1, 2018, and together they rocketed to worldwide recognition, with crushing results for men like Harvey Weinstein.

New Power authors Jeremy Heimans and Henry Timms illustrate the power shift when they refer to

Harvey Weinstein. Here's a man who had incredible control over rising young stars in Hollywood.
He played the lecher in the age-old casting couch
story — dozens of women have come forward with
allegations of sexual misconduct against him
(though these have yet to be proven in court). In
the majority of cases, he promised the actors film
roles and threatened them with banishment if they
dared to blow the whistle. He literally made many
careers with his position and power. But then the
curtain fell on Weinstein and his career. Heimans
and Timms recount how Weinstein was thanked
award season after award season while he "ruled
over Hollywood like a God. In fact, between 1966
and 2016, he actually *tied* with God for the total
number of times each was thanked in acceptance
speeches on Oscar night — thirty-four."

Another sign of the times was when Amnesty
International announced that its 2018 Rights Today
report, titled "Why Our Movement Matters," would
be devoted entirely to women's rights: "Women
around the world have been at the forefront of the
battle for human rights in 2018." The summary of
women-led events that year reads like a manifesto:

In India and South Africa, thousands took to
the streets to protest against endemic sexual
violence. In Saudi Arabia and Iran respec-
tively, women activists risked arrest to resist
the driving ban and forced *hijab* (veiling). In
Argentina, Ireland and Poland, demonstra-
tors rallied in vast numbers to demand an
end to oppressive abortion laws. Millions
of people in the USA, Europe, and parts of
Asia joined #MeToo-led women's marches
to demand an end to misogyny and abuse.
In northeastern Nigeria, thousands of displaced women mobilized for justice for the
abuses they have suffered at the hands of
Boko Haram fighters and the Nigerian security forces . . . Citizens of Ireland voted by a
landslide to overturn the abortion ban . . . In
Iceland and Sweden, new laws were passed
recognizing sex without consent as rape.

Also that year, India banned Islamic instant
divorce. And Canada's Prime Minister Justin
Trudeau maintained the position that trade nego-
tiations must include gender equality protection.
And Iceland announced that any company that
paid women less than men for doing the same job

would be fined. A year earlier, in 2017, Lebanon repealed the law that gave a rapist impunity if he married the victim; so did El Salvador. Chile relaxed its abortion law. Norway announced that the women's soccer team would be paid the same as the men's team. But all the good news does not diminish the distance women and girls still have to travel: nine-year-old girls are still being married off to sixty-year-old men; in many parts of the world, girls are still being denied an education; and violence against women continues to be a scourge throughout the world.

And still there are those who see the rise of women as the fall of men. I remember Dr. Sima Samar, the director of the Afghanistan Independent Human Rights Commission, saying, "Men in Afghanistan think that if women have equality it must mean men have to give their equality away." It's an odd notion that may go a long way in explaining the reluctance of some men to share the podium with women. In spite of the indisputable evidence that says the economy will improve and poverty and violence will be reduced if men and women both sit at the policy table, there continue to be those who see women as decoration, as sex slaves, as some sort of "other" — and some of them occupy the White House.

Women have always been subject to a bizarre duality that sees them on the one hand as fragile creatures who need protection, and on the other as evil Jezebels from whom society needs protection. A mullah in Bangladesh judges a woman indecent because she wants to work and earn money to feed her children. A judge in Canada finds a man not guilty of sexual assault because the woman he attacked was "not exactly wearing a bonnet and crinolines." The woman in Bangladesh is ostracized. The woman in Canada is ridiculed.

Until very recently, the natural order of society has fallen to patriarchy. Women in Africa, in Asia, and in the Americas tend to be identified with feelings rather than reason, with their bodies rather than their minds. So it is often the case that the girl child is victimized by the same misogyny that affects her mother. She's fed last and least. She's denied education and saddled with the responsibility of household chores while her brothers go out and play. In India, female babies aren't wanted and are sometimes starved to death so families can avoid financially crushing dowry payments; girls are burned to death as teenage brides because their husbands want to get rid of them for a better dowry. In China during the one-child rule, the number of baby girls who were abandoned or dropped to their death from towers skyrocketed because society puts greater value on boys. In Peru and Mexico, girls are sold into slavery, and in Bangladesh they're sometimes told at the tender age of five or six to leave home and make their own way in the world. They join thousands of other girls in the streets, looking for something to eat, trying to stay alive. And in Canada and the U.S., where women boast charter rights and equality under the law, more than one-third of the street kids are girls, and most of them are there because they're running away from abuse — usually sexual abuse at home.

Studies done back in 1985 by the World Bank proved that investing in the girl child is profitable. If she gets enough to eat, some education (so she can read and write), and minimal health care, three things will happen: she'll marry later, she'll have fewer children, and those children will be healthier. Economists claim that this change alone can eradicate poverty in the village, save the environment, and put the country to work. The World Bank has continued to follow the status of girls and its effect on the economy. According to its 2018 report, if girls face limits to their educational opportunities and barriers to finishing twelve full years of education, that deprivation costs their countries between $15 trillion and $30 trillion in earnings and lifetime productivity. World Bank CEO Kristalina Georgieva says, "We cannot keep letting gender inequality get in the way of global progress. Inequality in education is yet another fixable issue that is costing the world trillions. It is time to close the gender gap in education and give girls and boys an equal chance to succeed, for the good of everyone."

THERE'S AN IRONIC and heartwarming example of the journey that women have been travelling. It tells a little like a whodunnit. It is about a Fearless Girl in New York City. She's in fact a bronze statue that appeared, all four feet of her, the day before International Women's Day in March 2017, at the narrow end of Bowling Green park. She stood there — hands on hips, chest thrust forward, ponytail slightly askew, as though defying the 3.5-ton, eighteen-foot-long charging bronze bull that's been staring down New Yorkers since December 15, 1989.

Fearless Girl became the new kid on the block and an instant hit. She was placed there to celebrate the first anniversary of the Gender Diversity Index on the New York Stock Exchange. But the artist who sculpted *Charging Bull*, one Arturo Di Modica, was furious that some girl was taking on his bull, belittling the beast that had squatting rights at the park. He called it an "advertising trick." A friend of his even sculpted a dog peeing on the leg of *Fearless Girl*.

The fight was on.

Di Modica demanded that *Fearless Girl* be removed. State Street Global Advisors, the investment management firm that put her there, said their goal was "to raise awareness about the importance of gender diversity in corporate leadership." They boasted that in the six months following the unveiling of *Fearless Girl*, more than three hundred companies added women to their boards of directors. A tall claim, especially for a company that was found wanting when it came to being scrutinized by NPR's Camila Domonoske, who reported in October 2017 that according to a Department of Labour investigation, State Street Global Advisors regularly underpaid female and Black executives.

Like other breathtaking denouements, this one wound up on Twitter, and the conversation seemed to reflect the women's movement itself. "Keep her," tweeted most. "Move her," demanded a few, with an eye to the traffic on the busy corner. A year later, in April 2018, word filtered down from Mayor Bill de Blasio's office that *Fearless Girl* was going to be moved to the front of the New York Stock Exchange. So was *Charging Bull*. It appeared that the duel between the bronzes had ended in a draw. On November 28, when *Fearless Girl* was moved from her original location, a pair of footprints was left behind with a sign that read: "Fearless Girl is on the move to the New York Stock Exchange. Until she's there, stand in for her." On December 10, she landed in her new place and was greeted by Betty Liu, the executive vice-chairwoman of the New York Stock Exchange. Seven months before *Fearless Girl* arrived, the New York Stock Exchange had appointed Stacey Cunningham as its first female president in 226 years. Bet she'd been waiting for *Fearless Girl* to join her.

It's a cautionary tale to the world. Like the handprints on the ancient cave walls, it cries out, "We're here. This is our turf as well as yours."

It does indeed take a meeting of tectonic plates to move a file as big as women's rights, as big as half the world's population. For thirty years I've been out there recording, watching, telling — calling out the good and the evil stories. I am a witness to the violence, the hatred, and the prejudice of the Taliban, of Boko Haram, of ISIS, of two-bit thugs like Donald Trump and the presidents of the Philippines, Poland, Hungary, Saudi Arabia, Egypt, and Turkey. I am also a witness to the extraordinary courage of women who say, "Never again, not my daughter." Who say, "Time's up." Who say, "Me too." Who say, "Yes, I can." The misogynists who have targeted women and the notion of equality throughout history may think they are still in the game when they rush in against the wave of populist movements and attack women's progress as though it impedes the lives of men. They aren't. This story isn't just about men making room for women or women catching up to men. It's about the future.

- One in three women experiences some form of physical or sexual abuse in her lifetime.
- At least 200 million women and girls alive today have been subjected to female genital mutilation and its many complications.
- Women and girls account for 72 percent of global human trafficking victims, and more than three-quarters are trafficked for the purpose of sexual exploitation.

- The cost of intimate partner violence globally is about $4.4 trillion dollars, approximately 5.2 percent of the global GDP.
- The International Labour Organization pegs the labour force participation rate for women at 49 percent, while for men it's 75 percent.
- More than 2.7 billion women are legally prevented from having the same employment options as men, and 104 economies have laws preventing women from working specific jobs.
- Of those women included in the workforce, many are overrepresented in the bottom third of overall earnings. And women continue to be underrepresented across the board in executive and decision-making positions.
- Despite a gradual narrowing of the global gender pay gap over time, there is on average a 32 percent gap between men and women, and even within the OECD, the average hovers around 18 percent. This, by the way, has worsened somewhat since 2016.
- Even those women who are high-earning, who feature in the top 1 percent — their male counterparts are earning nearly twice as much.

- Women of all ages are more likely than men to live in poverty, and the majority of the 1.2 billion people living on less than $1.25 a day are women.

- According to UN Women, primary-aged girls are twice as likely to be out of school as boys.

- Many governments show open support for policies and laws that oppress women.

- Forty percent of women of childbearing age live in jurisdictions that severely restrict abortion, and 225 million don't have access to modern contraception.

- Funding cuts to family planning clinics in the U.S. have endangered the health of millions of women.

- In July 2018, Bulgaria ruled that the Istanbul Convention, a European treaty designed to fight domestic violence and violence against women, was "unconstitutional," and declined to ratify it.

- Reportedly, one in ten girls will be sexually assaulted before the age of twenty; only one-third of EU countries acknowledge non-consensual sex as rape.

- In Somalia, women with disabilities are

frequently forced into marriages and subjected to domestic violence.

- In Canada, Indigenous women are six times
  likelier than other women to be murdered.
- In Latin America and Europe, anti-rights
  groups have labelled feminists and LGBTQ
  activists "proponents of gender ideology"
  and claimed that they imperil "marriage and
  family values."
- Because of their reliance on social security
  benefits, women in the U.K. reportedly bear
  86 percent of the burden brought about by
  austerity measures since 2010.
- Currently, only 17 percent of all heads of
  state or government, and 23 percent of the
  world's parliamentarians, are women.

CHAPTER TWO

THE MATING GAME

LET'S TALK ABOUT SEX: sex for pleasure, for love, for procreation, for health, for punishment, for victory, for genocide, for marketing, for sales; it is a vast and complicated subject. We've gone from goddesses who give birth to the object of derision, from chastity belts to rape kits, from flirting to sexting, from being invisible in the anthropological research to being feted with bronze statues. And we have made our own choices as straight, lesbian, trans, and queer. After the cave dwellers and the hunters and gatherers and the Greeks and Romans and then the Industrial Revolution, the Enlightenment period, the Victorians, and all who followed, this era might well be called the Time of the Changemakers. There isn't a sexual behaviour — from soldiers raping and pillaging in victory to movie moguls sexually assaulting young stars to fathers marrying off young girls to avoid shame, to free love and free choice of lover — that isn't under the microscope today. Even Adam and Eve are being revisited.

THE STORY OF ADAM AND EVE makes up only a few verses in the book of Genesis, yet it has affected three major religions and clung to civilization for two thousand years as a morality play about fear and desire. Most of the world bought into the interpretation that he ate the forbidden fruit but she talked him into the transgression, so she must be the evil one. In *The Rise and Fall of Adam and Eve*, the American author and historian Stephen Greenblatt writes about Arcangela Tarabotti, a seventeenth-century Italian nun whose book *Paternal Tyranny* was posthumously published in 1654. Considered by many scholars to be a proto-feminist and early political theorist, Tarabotti was a sharp-witted and sharp-tongued woman who wanted a formal education and an independent life in the literary circles of Venice but was forced by her father at the age of sixteen into confinement in a

Benedictine convent. She got her revenge by writing about the injustices perpetrated against women, accusing parents of treating convents as dumping grounds for disabled, illegitimate, or otherwise unwanted daughters. She also turned her considerable powers of analysis to books she thought to be misogynist, including the Adam and Eve story in the Bible. Women, she argued, are men's equals in God's eyes.

Greenblatt refers to Tarabotti's description of the Adam and Eve story as "a scathing indictment of the cruelty that led to the misery that she and others like her suffered and an indictment too of the lies men used to justify this cruelty." According to Tarabotti, there was no inequality of the sexes in Eden, and what's more, she says, men have used violence and deceit to oppress women. While the Bible says woman was led astray by the devil in serpent form, Tarabotti retells the story, quoting God as saying to Eve: "Truly the devil stands for the male, who from now on will cast on to you the blame for his failings and will have no other purpose than deceiving you, betraying you, and removing all your rights of dominion granted by my omnipotence."

Tarabotti's views on the Adam and Eve story

were shared, if less vociferously, more than two centuries earlier, in 1405, by Christine de Pizan, who wrote, "Man and woman should be glad for this sin" in her book *Le Livre de la cité des dames*. And more than a century after the publication of *Paternal Tyranny*, Mary Wollstonecraft wrote satirically in *A Vindication of the Rights of Women*, "Probably the prevailing opinion that woman was created for man, may have taken its rise from Moses' poetical story." Needless to say, Tarabotti's work was attacked, condemned, and banned, and her writing was largely ignored until the twentieth century. "The taint of misogyny [regarding Eve] remained," says Greenblatt, "like the bitter residue in a cask one can never completely scrub clean."

That's the confounding thing about women's rights. The oppression that began ten thousand years ago is sustained through the ages with that "bitter residue." And, as Sonny and Cher sang, the beat goes on—and on—and on.

The Biblical creation story of Adam and Eve jostles uncomfortably with the lives of those who lived before the Old Testament was written—the people of the Stone Age, who weren't worrying about original sin or even restricting their partnerships to one man and one woman. New research suggests

that monogamy is actually a fairly new phenomenon that came at the end of the hunter-gatherer
period, about ten thousand years ago, when people
began to own land and farm their own crops. Before
that, say Christopher Ryan and Cacilda Jethá, the
authors of *Sex at Dawn: The Prehistoric Origins of
Modern Sexuality*, hunter-gatherer human beings
shared resources like food and child care — and sexual interaction.

The field of evolutionary psychology, claim
the authors, has been tainted by biases concerning sexuality. They use the term "Flintstonization"
to describe the projection of contemporary
assumptions onto early societies — including the
assumption that our species is primarily monogamous. Prior to the onset of the agricultural era, they
contend, humans were more promiscuous and less
concerned with paternity. And they claim that sexual interactions strengthened the bond of trust in
the groups; playful sexual interactions, rather than
provoking jealousy, benefited social equilibrium.

The implications go beyond sexual behaviour,
suggesting that humans are egalitarian and selfless
overall. In an interview on the program *Equal Time
for Freethought* on the New York radio station WBAI,
Ryan explained, "We're not saying that sharing was

so widespread because everyone was loving and sitting around the fire singing 'Kumbaya' every night. The reason that sharing was so widespread — and continues to be in the remaining hunter-gatherer societies in existence — is because it's simply the most efficient way of distributing risk among a group of people."

So, according to this research, we moved from promiscuity being rampant to monogamy being *de rigueur*, and from egalitarian relationships to patriarchy, about ten thousand years ago. The short answer for why monogamy took hold is: no one really knows. But anthropologists postulate that as agriculture developed and groups of people living together grew larger because of an abundance of food, offspring became increasingly important as future labourers. So protecting the pregnant woman, as well as the pregnancy and the offspring, from others in the group resulted in monogamous relationships, and that was the undercurrent of the history that followed — although the evolutionary anthropologist Kit Opie thinks that today we may be moving away from monogamy.

But none of that explains the lingering connection to Adam and Eve or the purity demanded of women and their bodies. For example, anthropologists have discovered that some statues of voluptuous, big-breasted women have actually had breast reductions! Doris Couture-Rigert, chief of conservation at the National Gallery of Canada, in Ottawa, could hardly believe her eyes when in 2019 she spied a change in the gilding of a Madonna statue and realized modifications had been made to the breast area. "I examined other works and found the same phenomenon on some, which led me to wonder how widespread this was and where it was happening," she says. She has only just begun her study and expects to find further evidence in Europe, but she already knows the carving down of women's breasts on sculptures was done during the nineteenth century and more specifically during the Victorian era, when the showing of large breasts was no longer seen as proper. So far, her examinations have concentrated on Madonna sculptures in Catholic churches in Quebec.

"What drew my attention was the change of the surface texture below the surface finish. It was barely perceptible, but I could see that the texture below the gilding had changed," she says. Microscopic examination and cross-section analysis indeed revealed that the statue had been altered by locally recarving the wood and then re-gilding.

Who did the breast reduction, she says, is not as relevant as who commissioned it — presumably the Catholic Church. "Look at the Baroque period, when everything was lavish and sometimes over the top and maybe too loose, eventually forcing the pendulum to swing into the opposite direction," she says. "As a result, the Victorian era that followed was very proper, and we have to conclude that this influenced the priests to pay someone to alter the original and render the statue to what was perceived as more proper."

With so much new data having come from women researchers, I asked Couture-Rigert if this work might have been overlooked by a male conservator. She said, "I believe women see things through their own lens, and that enriches the traditional male lens. However, noticing this surface change on a sculpture, which led to the discovery of this phenomenon, is not linked to the gender of the conservator. It was simply the result of a thorough, in-depth examination."

It's quite remarkable that even the Madonna had to be sculpted to meet the expectations of the time. Like the "fallen Eve" story, this presents a picture of women who need to be altered to be accepted. Being less or second or not considered at all, or being left out or inferior — which also means imperfect and substandard and, as if that's not enough, evil — is the way half the world's population was objectified. John Stuart Mill wrote that such objectification caused women to develop artificially submissive personalities, which degraded not only them but also the men who objectified them.

Apart from the philosophical and emotional aspects of being cast as less valuable, that dismissal builds societal systems and structures that reinforce the power imbalance we are trying to sort out today.

Quick, take this test. Picture this person in your mind — doctor, lawyer, politician, scientist, CEO. Who did you see? Most say they picture a man. Or try this: picture these gender-neutral words — participant, user, researcher. Who do you see? Again, most see a man. The simple truth is the data we use for everything from medical tests to vehicle safety to office temperatures to snow removal is hopelessly biased.

For example, why would the medical profession decide not to include females while testing for heart attack symptoms and stroke symptoms? Why would they test drugs only on males? Researchers once claimed that women's menstrual cycles got in the way of accurate analysis. So their prevention, diagnosis, and treatment of disease was based on research done exclusively on men. It wasn't until doctors began to realize that heart attack and stroke symptoms are different for women than for men that the researchers in the labs had an "aha" moment that changed the way heart disease and strokes were studied, diagnosed, and treated.

It was that fact that convinced author Caroline Criado Perez to write her astonishing book *Invisible Women*, about a world that's been built for men. She exposed the gender data gap. For example:

- Women are 50 percent more likely than men to be misdiagnosed following a heart attack, and they are more likely to die.
- Office temperatures are set five degrees too cold for women, because the formula to determine temperature was developed in the 1960s, based on the resting metabolic rate of a forty-year-old man. Women's metabolic rates are slower, so they need more heat.
- The crash test dummy is traditionally male. Which means he is taller and heavier than most women. And that means safety designs for vehicles are flawed for women, who sit

closer to the pedals and whose pelvic cavities are in a position different to men's. And although seatbelts have been required since the 1970s, there still isn't a safe alternative for pregnant women. Statistics show women are 47 percent more likely than men to be seriously injured in a car accident, and 17 percent more likely to die.

- In Sweden, snow removal crews were challenged to justify why they removed snow from roads first and sidewalks last. Men tend to drive to work and women to take public transit (to work, to the children's school, to the grocery store, to daycare). Driving in three centimetres of snow is less dangerous than walking in it. The crews reversed the order and cleared the sidewalks first, saving money by preventing falls on icy sidewalks.
- Blind auditions have increased the proportion of female players hired by orchestras by 50 percent.
- Smartphones are 5.5 inches (14 centimetres) long—too big for most women's hands and certainly too big for our pockets.
- We know exactly how much weight a construction worker can safely carry, but we

have no idea what effect the fumes from nail polish remover have on mani-pedi workers.
- Women are ignored when they ask for work gloves small enough to fit their hands, military boots narrow enough to fit their feet, and bulletproof vests that account for breasts.

Criado Perez says we're used to seeing men as the default human, and she doesn't pull punches when she talks about how women got short-changed: "Most of recorded human history is one big data gap . . . the lives of all men have been taken to represent those of humans overall. When it comes to the lives of the other half of humanity, there is often nothing but silence."

Talking to Piya Chattopadhyay on CBC's *The Current*, she described a scintillating piece of research around a drug called sildenafil citrate, which showed potential during clinical trials for women suffering from menstrual cramps and pre-menstrual syndrome (PMS). The drug created an increase in blood flow to the pelvic region, which helped alleviate cramping but also gave researchers the idea that it ought to be tested on men with erectile disfunction. It became Viagra, the now famous little blue pill. But the shocking denouement is that when Viagra turned into a gold mine for pharmaceutical companies, the trials for medical relief of women's period pain and PMS were stopped. Researchers hoping to pursue that avenue have been denied funding "because it wasn't deemed a public health priority," said Perez. In fact, a search of titles and abstracts on the science social networking site ResearchGate found there were more than five times as many studies on erectile dysfunction as there were on PMS.

Today, medical researchers know that two-thirds of Alzheimer's patients are women and that an American woman's risk of developing the disease is twice that of a man. So hormonal changes at menopause and the use of household cleaning agents have now come under the microscope.

And imagine this: the much-heralded all-female spacewalk scheduled to take place Friday, March 29, 2019, had to be cancelled because one of the spacesuits was too big for one of the female astronauts. And dangling outside the capsule 322 kilometres above the earth for a six-hour mission in a suit that doesn't fit is not a good idea. So the spacewalk went ahead with one woman and one man, and the historic walk was scrubbed. It was supposed to be astronauts Anne McClain and Christina Koch, with ground crew member Mary Lawrence as flight director and Jackie Kagey as lead officer — a first all-women flight event. This brings new meaning to "man-made."

The gender data gap is entrenched in everything from algorithms developed in Silicon Valley with male-only data to literature and theatre. In beloved musicals like *My Fair Lady*, which premiered as a film on October 21, 1964, the character Henry Higgins sings about his protege, Eliza Doolittle, "Why can't a woman be more like a man?" And in popular movies like *The Sound of Music*, released on March 2, 1965, Liesl sings to her boyfriend, Rolfe, "I need someone older and wiser telling me what to do. You are seventeen going on eighteen, I'll depend on you."

Then, in 1967, the sexual status of women exploded on the public scene, and women sang the song written by the Brothers-in-Law exhorting listeners to "put all your faith in the pill." The infamous birth control pill ushered in a sexual revolution for women. What promise it offered: women could be sexually active without the fear of pregnancy; they could have control over the timing and spacing of their children. The pill was affordable, safe, and effective. The stage was set for what was then called Women's Liberation, better known as Women's Lib, which burst into the 1960s like an awakening. As women questioned the patriarchy and the control men had over their legal and physical lives, the pill also launched a furious backlash in the battle for equality. Some men, many clergy, and several bosses saw birth control as the cause of everything from promiscuity and infidelity to workplace shenanigans and a thrashing of family values. Indeed, it raised the socially acceptable age of marriage, and to the horror of most mothers, girls became sexually active at a younger age. But mostly the pill empowered women — to finish an education, to pursue a career, to plan their lives according to want as well as need.

Despite the freedom and independence ushered in by the Sixties, woman-as-sexual-target never ceased. "Sleeping around" and "having a bad rep" or being one of "those girls" were the new monikers for the fairer sex who put all their faith in the pill. In 1978, the author John Irving published *The World According to Garp*, a novel about T. S. Garp, born a bastard to a feminist leader who defied the social mores of her time. *The World According to Garp* opens with Garp's mother being sexually assaulted in a theatre, but no one believes her.

"I can hardly believe, forty years after my book was published, we still don't believe women who have been sexually assaulted," he said in an interview on CBC's Q in November 2018. His comment was prompted by President Donald Trump's controversial second nominee for the Supreme Court of the United States. Brett Kavanaugh's nomination had been challenged when psychology professor Christine Blasey Ford accused him of sexually assaulting her when they were teenagers. In late September 2018, both Ford and Kavanaugh testified before the Senate Judiciary Committee. Ford told the senators she was 100 percent certain that Kavanaugh sexually assaulted her in 1982. Kavanaugh furiously dismissed the allegations, accusing Democrats of a "calculated and orchestrated political hit" designed to keep him off the Supreme Court. At the end of the hearing, he won the position. Ford lost because they didn't believe her.

Irving told me in an interview that at a press conference in France for the fortieth anniversary of *The World According to Garp*, "a journalist asked me if I did not think *The World According to Garp* was bizarre in literature today; considered too outrageous that a woman is publicly assaulted and no one believes her." He came home from that trip in time to hear the Kavanaugh hearings. "If anyone doubts how women are treated, they only need to remember how the president of the United States mocked and ridiculed those who came forward against Judge Kavanaugh."

His reflections about a book he wrote four decades ago are telling. "When I was writing the novel," he told me in 2019, "I thought that this level of sexual intolerance and intolerance of difference and of minorities might mean I was in danger of writing a period piece — the fear women have of men, the hatred men have of women. *The World According to Garp* is about extremes of sex, hatred, and violence. I was exaggerating something that was true. It doesn't seem as exaggerated today as it seemed when I wrote it. In the midst of so-called sexual liberation, both gay and straight, I can't say things haven't improved; they have. Is there still intolerance? Yes. Are women still treated as a sexual minority? Yes."

Irving's novel *The Cider House Rules* also addressed women and society, treading the delicate territory of abortion. Published in 1985, the novel follows Wilbur Larch, an obstetrician and founder and director of an orphanage in rural Maine in the pre- and postwar eras. The doctor is a saint. He is also an ether addict and an abortionist. And it's about his protege, the orphan Homer Wells, who follows Larch's footsteps and struggles with his own conscience. Irving's account of researching the book, which became an Academy Award–winning film in 1999, is also an account, both tender and disturbingly honest, of the lives of girls and women. He remembers that when he was in grade seven, a girl in his class disappeared. She didn't come back until the following year and had to repeat the grade. He asked his mom what might have happened to her. She suggested the girl might have gone to the orphanage. He didn't know what that meant and didn't ask. Much later, when he was doing research at the Medical Historical Library at Yale University for the *The Cider House Rules*, he read about orphanages in New England, including one called the New England Home for Little Wanderers. He began to understand that this was a place where unwed women went to have babies. Examining photos from 1934 and 1940, he saw the same nurses and doctors and the same children, but the kids in the first photo were older in the second.

"I realized no one took the older ones," he said. "They only took the babies. One night after that, I called my mother and asked her about the orphanage. 'Did you mean the girls went there to have a baby or to have an abortion?' I realized then that a girl who was out of school for a couple of weeks had probably had an abortion. If she was gone a year, she'd had a baby."

In a scene in the book, an abortion rights activist asks a doctor who refuses to perform the procedure, "If women have no choice, then why do you have choice?" The doctor says, "I don't have the right to decide until they have the right to decide." Years later, when the novel was being adapted for film, Irving insisted that it get a PG rating, because "Twelve- and thirteen-year-olds can and do get pregnant, and I wanted them to see this movie, to see when there was no safe, clean option — nothing in that story would happen if abortion was legal."

IN THE TIME FRAMES of John Irving's books, pregnant girls were sent away to distant and anonymous homes to have their babies, which were then adopted out. It was a form of silencing and erasing transgressions against the patriarchal code of conduct. That's the code women are challenging today. For example, the novelist Pat Barker has written an extraordinary book called *The Silence of the Girls*, retelling Homer's *Iliad* from the point of view of the women whose voices are absent from the Greek epic. Written in the mid-eighth century BCE, *The Iliad* — one of the most famous and beloved stories of all time — narrates the conclusion of the Greek siege of the city of Troy. Central to the conflict is a quarrel among the Greeks over whether Chryseis — a woman taken as a war prize and enslaved by Agamemnon, leader of the Greek forces — should be given back to her father, Chryses, a priest of Apollo. Agamemnon offends Apollo by threatening to ransom Chryseis instead, so the god inflicts a plague on the Greeks. The hero Achilles convinces the Greeks to make Agamemnon return Chryseis; in compensation, Agamemnon takes Achilles' own battle-trophy concubine, Briseis.

Barker provides the missing side of the story — the world of the women we usually see only as silent, subservient figures on plinths, eyes cast down and flowers in their hair. She gives voice to the silenced women in Greece and Rome, imagining what they would have said when they were alone with each other. For all the extraordinary brutality, the spurting blood and spilled guts, the voices of the women who speak behind their hands in the shadows of the rooms of Troy tell us how they felt about each other: about the smells and jealousies and fears about the violence that follows loss.

Like Homer's original, Barker's novel is about war, brutality, and the power of men — but from the point of view of the women who hated them, mocked them, and feared them. She shows how the fall of Troy utterly transforms the life of Briseis, who goes from queen to slave. "Here I was again," Briseis says, "waiting for Achilles to decide when it was time for bed, still trapped, still stuck inside his story, and yet with no real part to play in it."

The Iliad may be about war, but for Briseis it's about the horror of that time when the battle is won and the city is in flames and the streets are littered with the dead — "And then they turned their attention to us." She describes the night Achilles won her as a prize: "What can I say. He wasn't cruel. I waited for it, expected it, even — but there was nothing like that, and at least it was soon over. He fucked as quickly as he killed." She knows Achilles owns her and she has no recourse but to serve him. She recalls how, after her capture, she was passed around from man to man; and then, when she was being bartered for by Achilles, he tossed her back to her last keeper and said, "Tell him he can fuck her till her back breaks." And Briseis says, "I do what countless women before me have been forced to do. I spread my legs for the man who killed my husband and my brother."

Like the handprints of the women on the cave walls, Barker gives voice to women. "I was here," they say. "This happened to me."

CENTURIES AFTER HOMER wrote his epic poem, rape and the violence and power it asserts continue to wear many masks. Some scorch the victim's emotional earth, as women like Eva Penavic discovered in the Balkans during the civil war that raged through the first half of the 1990s. I met Eva in the early nineties, when I went back to Croatia and Bosnia, trying to find a woman who could testify to the rape camps. Twenty-five years later, Eva's daughter, Tatiana, and Eva's grandchildren, who had ranged in age from newborn to nine years old when I first met them and were now adults with children of their own, found me on Facebook. They remembered the many visits I had made to Vinkovci, where they had found shelter after being expelled from their home in Berak, Croatia, often late at night in the pitch black, to avoid the shelling. The house was two kilometres from the front line of the war. Bombs were exploding in the near distance, shaking the windows and lighting up the room. There were eleven people living in the house: Eva's sons and daughter, their spouses and children. Now the grandchildren wondered if I would come back and visit Eva and the family. They wanted me to know that the men who gang-raped their grandmother had never been arrested, never been charged with their terrible crime, and that they were still living in the same village, still passing Eva on the street, and still calling themselves citizens of Berak. After the war in Yugoslavia, similar atrocities followed in Rwanda, Congo, and Darfur, where tens of thousands of women were raped as an act of war. But to hear Eva's children and grandchildren tell me that nothing had been done to right the terrible wrongs committed against their beloved grandmother forced me to reckon with the historical resistance to establishing justice for rape victims, and the moral reprehension the families bear forever. From Homer's women to the women of Afghanistan and the Yazidi women and girls, the revolution for women has indeed been long, and the power shift includes a new generation — in this case, the grandchildren of Eva Penavic are taking on the battle.

I remember meeting Eva, worrying about telling her story and making it public. But she was adamant that the world know the truth. Through a translator, she said, "Until someone says, 'This is my name, this is my face, this is what you did to me,' we won't be able to have justice." Before the war ended and after she'd escaped the men who raped her, she and her family were living in a town near their home in Berak, which they had been forced to abandon. They all wondered about the farm, the crops, the animals, and who among their neighbours had managed to stay after Serbian soldiers, known as Chetniks, had chased so many people away. I had convinced a UN employee, whose job included checking on the towns the Croats had fled, to take me with him on one of his patrols. "Meet me at the Hotel Slavonia," he said. "Bring nothing but yourself." When Eva found out, she had frantically mixed feelings. She wanted desperately to know the state of her house and farmland, but she was also terrified that the Chetniks would catch me. She kept drawing her finger across her throat to warn me not to go. Later, I was able to tell her the name of the Serbian family who had been displaced from an area the Croats had taken and who were now living in Eva's home. She wanted every single detail about my time in Berak, and then shook her finger at me to say I should never have gone.

The crime committed against her was part of a plan, a cruel adjunct to the insidious campaign known as "ethnic cleansing," or genocide. The consequences of such crimes are not only the loss of several generations of women but also, perhaps, the annihilation of a race and culture. An estimated twenty thousand to forty thousand women shared Eva's fate.

I will never forget the story she told that first night at her house. The grandchildren had been put to bed; her own children sat in stark silence. It seemed as though everyone in the room was holding their breath. She spoke quietly at first, clutching her hands together, then smoothing invisible creases on her apron. At times she stood up, punching her fists into the air, shouting out an accusation, and then sitting down again and whispering the hideous facts of the crime. It was a bloodless bloodletting for her. It stays with me as though it happened yesterday. This, in part, is what I reported at the time:

Then they attacked her, like a pack of jack-
als. Six men stripped her, then raped her by
turns, orally and vaginally. They ejaculated
and urinated into her mouth. They screamed
that she was an old woman and if she was dry
they'd cut her vagina with knives and use
her blood to make her wet. She was chok-
ing on semen and urine and couldn't breathe.
The noise was horrendous as the six men
kept shrieking at her that there were twenty
more men waiting their turn and calling out,
"Who's next?" She was paralyzed with fear
and with excruciating pain. The assault continued relentlessly for three hours.

When they were finished with her they
dressed her, cleaned themselves off with her
lingerie and stuffed the fouled underwear
into her mouth, demanding she eat it. Then
they marched her back outside into the garden and pushed her into the cornfield behind
the house and told her to run away. She knew
the field was mined. She stumbled through the
slushy snow and sharp cornstalks. Then she
slipped in the muddy field and fell and at
exactly that moment bullets ripped over her
head. She flattened herself into the mud as

she heard the cheers of the terrorists who thought they had bagged another kill.

Eva got away. She found her missing sons — one had been in hiding, the other detained in a camp with other prisoners. And her daughter, daughters-in-law, and grandchildren had been hidden away in a safe town. They never found her husband's body. That terrible time in the life of the matriarch lingers. Like most families on the other side of catastrophe, they rebuilt their lives and eventually recovered their house and barns and farm fields. The countryside surrounding the village still resembles a mural crayoned by children, with a clutch of white stucco houses with clay tile roofs and a few barns. On one side of the village is a patchwork of rolling hills and a thick oak forest so green and purple and yellow that the colours could have been splashed there by rainbows; on the other side are stretches of flat black farmland with rows of venerable old trees. The town itself is an antique treasure, a three-hundred-year-old tableau of muted colours and softly worn edges — an unlikely setting for the ugliness that happened here in 1992.

When I got the email from Eva's grandchildren, I

was delighted to see their faces and read their news. But when they told me they were still seeking justice for their grandmother, I was astonished. After all this — the gang-raping of women, the international intervention, the famed Dayton Accords that brought an end to the bloodshed — there was no justice for those who had been harmed? These people I met as babies and toddlers and young people are now adults who know the tyranny of the past and are demanding accountability today.

Invariably when I meet women in war zones, as I have done for thirty years, our conversation, sometimes through an interpreter, sometimes in English, takes place at the cookstove or the firepit or while fetching water at the river, or in the village meeting house, where the walls are papered with kids' drawings and to-do lists and lofty posters about living life well. And invariably the conversation is about the issues they face because they are women, and the need for change: we have to build a school for girls; birth control needs to be available to us; women must run for public office. And even the kids are announcing their plans for tomorrow. At a school in Jaghori, in the central highlands of Afghanistan, where the Taliban forbade education for girls for five long years, the blond hair of an eleven-year-old called Wahida was peeking out of her head scarf and falling over her green eyes while she told me she wanted to be an astronaut when she grew up. And another child, six-year-old Parwana, with enormous brown eyes and jet-black hair tucked under her white head scarf, said, "When I'm grown up, I'm going to be somebody." And who might that somebody be, I asked her. She replied with aplomb, "The president of Afghanistan."

From September 26, 1996, to October 7, 2001, the "holy warriors" ruling Afghanistan had no theological misgivings about violating women and girls. Previously, under the mujahedeen, rape, abduction, and forced marriages had been commonplace, but the Taliban legally sanctioned this brutality. Women whispered about the abuse, but it was only after the Taliban were driven from Kabul that organizations like Human Rights Watch were able to document their stories. To the Taliban, women and girls were spoils of war, kept as concubines or sold as sex slaves, with the profits fuelling the war machine. Victims could not speak up for fear of execution. They couldn't even confide in family members, because of "honour": a defiled woman has dishonoured her family and must die.

A similarly warped philosophy saw ISIS take

five thousand Yazidi women and girls as sex slaves during the conflict in Iraq that began on August 3, 2014, when they attacked Shingal Mountain, a one-hundred-kilometre-long stretch of land that's been home to the Yazidis for eight thousand years. I met two Yazidi girls, thirteen-year-old Beshra and fourteen-year-old Badia, who had been captured by ISIS and held as sex slaves. They had managed to escape their captors and reunite with their mother and brothers and baby sister — their father was still being held by ISIS — in the Kabato refugee camp near Duhok in Northern Iraq, where they and fifteen thousand other Yazidis sheltered from the forty-seven-degree-Celsius heat in white UN tents pitched on gravel. When ISIS stormed into Shingal (called Sinjar by Arabs), the family was put under house arrest for nine days. They were told to convert to Islam or the men would be killed and the women and girls given to fighters.

"We converted, but we knew it would not mean we were safe," said Beshra. Soon they endured the same ritualistic capture as the other Yazidis: the men and boys were separated from the women and girls; the younger and prettiest girls were selected to be sex slaves; the men were taken away; the older women were left behind. The younger girls were told to take showers. They knew what was coming. One girl slit her wrists and bled to death on the floor of the showers. Beshra, Badia, and their cousin were taken to Syria.

"There I became a sex slave and was raped by a different fighter every day," said Beshra. Later, they were sold to fighters in two different towns. "The man who bought me is an Iraqi called Arkan," she said. "His nickname — they all had pseudonyms — was Abu Sarhan. But he lived with fifteen men. They raped me and my cousin whenever they wanted to and said we were their slaves."

One day, when the men were praying, Beshra and her cousin decided to flee. "We told the one left to guard us that we were going to the toilet. It was 5:15 a.m. We crept out of the house and started to run. Whenever we suspected movement, we hid in empty houses and waited for the road to be clear. When we started it was barely light enough for us to see our way. We ran and hid and kept running and hiding until we got to the paved road. Then we hid in the grasses at the side of the road until at last we saw peshmerga soldiers, who took us to Shingal Mountain." It was dark by the time the soldiers found the girls' families in the refugee camp.

Her sister, Badia, who managed to escape with

the help of a shepherd and rejoined the family a year after Beshra, described the isis fighters as "dirty, filthy men with huge scraggly beards who are always shouting, always angry, always stinking. They kicked us, raped us, did things to us I cannot describe, as I have never heard of them before."

Six months after I wrote their story for *Maclean's* magazine, Beshra and Badia managed to get a message to me from a mobile phone. "Come back," they said. "We're going to go home to Shingal Mountain; we want you to come with us." I thought it would be a meaningful story — the journey home after three years of hell. I went back to Iraq with photographer Peter Bregg, hoping we could accompany the girls on their emotional journey.

In this hardscrabble part of old Mesopotamia, modern architecture sits alongside cement-block houses on rocky hills with scrub growing from thin topsoil. We drove toward Shingal Mountain shortly after dawn. The checkpoints were busy with trucks hauling cauliflower, tomatoes, onions, and dates. Long-haired sheep in the backs of pickups bleated while grim guards checked papers. Deals were made; many vehicles were turned back. We had been told that getting through this checkpoint was a major hurdle; after that, our chances of reaching Shingal improved. Every insurgent group in Iraq was in these hills — ISIS, Al Qaeda, the PKK (the Kurdistan Workers' Party from Turkey, condemned by some as terrorists but hailed by others as rescuers).

The road beyond the checkpoint was lined with scattered villages: some Christian, marked with crosses on churches; some Arabic, with minarets by mosques; some Kurdish; some Armenian. We passed oil wells near the Syrian border. Absolute destruction lay ahead, the aftermath of revenge — it's not enough for advancing armies to destroy infrastructure; they will continue firing until the past is obliterated. Shingal was flattened and hauntingly empty. ISIS still lurked around the perimeter.

There was no way those girls could go back home. They must have known that, so why did they send the message? I soon figured it out. They had become their own change agents. They wanted to know if the world believed their story, if anyone was serious about rescuing them. If I came back, they'd take that as a sign that their truth would prevail. The girls were overjoyed when they saw us. They welcomed us into the tent where we'd met before — a tent that was home to eight people. They had cleverly rigged up an additional space by tying a tarp over poles at the door of the tent and extending it outwards to another pair of poles, creating a roof so they could cook outside. The place was spotless; it held the barest necessities — thin cushions to sit on, a cradle for the baby, a stack of quilts for when the cushions were transformed from chair to bed, and a small heater and a single light hanging from a wire. They poured us tea and offered us sweets and a place by the heater because it was bitterly cold and snowing outside. Everyone gathered around, mother, brothers, and baby sister, while Badia and Beshra told their terrible story, this time into a CBC microphone for *The Current*, and the teapot was passed and refilled and passed again.

Both of the girls were illiterate, but they were enthusiastic and thoughtful teenagers who knew they needed to find their way to a brighter future. They told me they longed to know how to write their names and read books. They also said they would not leave the camp until their father was released. They knew the likelihood that he'd been killed by ISIS was high, but accepting that fact was not useful now. In such a bleak place — displaced, living in a tent, worrying about the fate of their father — they shone an extraordinary light of hope.

They were not the victims ISIS had tried to make of them. They were imagining their garden, where they played as kids and planted their vegetables, and they wondered what was left of their home and what tomorrow would bring.

"I hope someday I will tell this story in a court, in front of all the world, so they will know what those men did to us," Beshra said.

Other refugees in Duhok confirmed ISIS's horrifying modus operandi. A twelve-year-old former sex slave said her owner used to tie her up at the end of his prayer rug. He would bow to the east, prostrate himself, and pray. And then he would turn around, untie her, and rape her. Older women shared tales of unspeakable brutality and dangerous dead-of-night escapes, sneaking past sleeping guards and out windows and sheltering in shepherds' huts, only to be betrayed and recaptured. Like Eva's grandchildren, they wanted accountability and wouldn't rest until they got it.

In 2016, I had the opportunity to interview six captured ISIS fighters in Duhok. The image I had of them was what I had seen on TV — men with huge black beards (I wondered whether they backcombed them to look more ferocious), wearing voluminous black clothing that made them look more like Darth Vader than warriors, marching down the street shouldering machine guns and swaggering through the villages, scaring people to death. Once they are in prison, they have to shave their beards and wear jeans and a T-shirt and a brown vest. So when I met the beasts who had committed hideous crimes against humanity, they looked more like hotel management students.

The prison in Duhok was painted white — the ceiling, walls, floor, even the bars of the cells were white. There were auto shops, wood shops, metal shops, gardens; they even had to sew their own garments. There were Ping-Pong tables and classrooms and what they call psych-social classes to deal with the behaviour that had gotten them there. The director of the prison had travelled to Europe to learn about prisons with rehabilitation programs and had modelled his institution after them.

The interviews I did revealed the barbarous attitude of the men who took those girls. "Every fighter is entitled to four girls," one brazen young prisoner said. I asked them why they took girls as sex slaves. They shrugged. I asked one of them if he would kill me. At first he said no, because Islam isn't about killing; but when pressed, he said ISIS would. One young man, whose job was to distribute the girls to the ISIS soldiers, was trying to cut himself a deal. When I showed him a photo of one of the missing girls and asked him if he recognized her, he said, "Get me out of here and I'll take you to her." At the end of the interview, the Yazidi man who had been translating stood facing him, almost nose to nose, and said, "I was there on Shingal Mountain when you attacked us. I don't hate you." The kid was speechless. He had tears in his eyes when the guard led him away.

IT HAS BEEN WELL ESTABLISHED that rape is about power. The power to punish, as Eva Penavic suffered; the power of the victor, as Homer's women experienced as war prizes; and for the Yazidi girls, the power to subjugate and destroy a people who have lived on a land for eight thousand years.

Three years before the #MeToo movement, news broke that the popular Canadian radio host Jian Ghomeshi was accused of assaulting women in the name of rough sex. Then he was accused of intimidating his female colleagues at work with comments such as "I want to hate-fuck you." Three women said he'd had sex with them without their consent. The case went to court and was headline news for months. He was acquitted on all but one of the charges, and the other was dismissed after he made a peace bond with his accuser. Still, on that Sunday in October 2014 when the first allegations surfaced, a taboo was lifted. The conversation that consumed the country over the subsequent days could have inspired significant change, affecting the horrific prevalence of sexual assault and sexual intimidation in the workplace and reducing the enormous economic cost of violence against women in Canada — $7.4 billion for spousal violence alone, according to the Canadian Women's Foundation.

But it didn't.

For centuries, men who commit sexual violence have gone unpunished. But their victims receive a life sentence. Silence and shame help perpetrators escape justice. Women know that the stigma of speaking up could cost them jobs, friendships, partnerships. And if they do go to court, it will be their sexual history that goes on trial. During the Ghomeshi case, that was reversed as the blogosphere offered loving support for the women who spoke. Then, on October 30, retired *Toronto Star* reporter Antonia Zerbisias and her Montreal friend Sue Montgomery, a justice reporter from the *Gazette*, tweeted #beenrapedneverreported. The hashtag went viral. Eight million people around the world joined Canadian women to say, "Enough." It was the single silver lining to that sordid affair.

Earlier, in 2013, stories had emerged about university initiations in the U.S., Canada, and elsewhere involving sexual harassment and rape. Women recognized this as evidence of a pervasive rape culture: a new, acceptable way of demeaning and sidelining women with that old adage "boys will be boys."

Like so many of the beginnings that came before, #beenrapedneverreported ran out of steam before the job was done. While it's unfair to say women slid backwards, it's accurate to say reform was stalled. Then Kirby Dick's documentary *The Hunting Ground* premiered at the Sundance Film Festival in 2015. University campuses in the U.S. are rife with accusations of date rape. Kirby brought them together into a nationwide examination of the causes and consequences of date rape, but more than that, he exposed the cover-up that protected the perpetrators. The documentary was a nominee at the 2016 Academy Awards.

Female victims, especially young ones, are easily dismissed — you were drunk, you can't remember the details, you were dressed like a tramp, you should have stayed in your dorm room. Kirby Dick went to the source — to the girls on campus who had a story to tell and rape kits to prove their accusations. What he found was a shameful cover-up carefully knit together by the very people responsible for keeping students safe. When questioned about the disturbing rate of rape on campus, the presidents and CEOs and registrars and provosts vehemently denied such behaviour in their hallowed halls, to avoid jeopardizing funding from donors. They even admonished the girls who dared to come forward.

The film opens with Erica Kinsman, a student at Florida State University, who recounts being raped at a party by the quarterback of the university football team, Jameis Winston. She reported the sexual assault to the police and the university student department. Her complaint was ignored. As a result of the systemic cover-up, young women from coast to coast shared their stories on social media. Then two women from the University of North Carolina, who had also been raped and ignored, filed a Title IX complaint (the U.S. law that says no one can be discriminated against in an educational program that receives federal financial assistance), which inspired women at other universities. But the documentary ends with a disturbing reminder that power and money too often beat out justice and safety: Jameis Winston was drafted first over-all by the NFL's Tampa Bay Buccaneers. The same man who was dealt a one-game suspension in 2014 for shouting "Fuck her right in the pussy" while standing on a table at the student union. The same man who was suspended for three games by the NFL on a charge of groping an Uber driver in 2016. Erica Kinsman's case against him was settled out of court, but the university paid her $950,000 to set-tle her lawsuit alleging a violation of Title IX and agreed to conduct five years of sexual awareness programs. As for Winston, he's still playing for the Buccaneers and will earn $21 million in 2019.

Although Kirby Dick was criticized by several universities and some news outlets for careless reporting, he said that his research showed that less than 8 percent of the population is respon-sible for 90 percent of sexual assaults. The point he was trying to make in the film and afterwards was this: unless the perpetrators are arrested, they will reoffend.

As awareness of rape culture increased, women from Nairobi to New York and from Mexico to Ukraine shared their experiences of being struck, choked, menaced, groped. A few years earlier, in March 2011, a group called Young Women for Change (YWC) was formed in Afghanistan to address the persistently disgraceful treatment women and girls receive on the streets of Kabul. Men call them names — whore, harlot, tramp; they grab their buttocks, push them aside simply because they are walking in public. The YWC decided to hit the streets and go public to gain support, marching with posters that demanded rights for women. They also opened an internet café so that women would have a safe place to go online, and they named it Sahar Gul, for the fifteen-year-old Afghan girl who was brutally beaten by her husband and his family when she refused to become a prostitute to bring money to them. Sahar is safe now, and the people who harmed her have been charged by the police, but the YWC want everyone to remember what can happen, so they will work to stop the violence and abuse of women. Co-founder Anita Haidary made a film called *My City Too* that included vivid examples of the street harassment and interviews about the consequences of treating women as though they don't belong. I attended the premier of the film in Kabul and was delighted to see that the hall was packed with young men and young women. I had already met a lot of them in YWC's cramped office quarters, where I was astonished to discover that half the members were young men. When I asked why, they responded, "We'll never get to the finish line unless we walk together." The organization epitomizes the effectiveness of speaking out. In fact, I even wear one of their T-shirts, which says, first in Dari and then in English, "A strong woman stands up for herself; a stronger woman stands up for the rights of all women."

Later the same year, on assignment in Cairo during the Tahrir Square protest against the Egyptian government, I visited the Nazra Center for Feminist Studies and found exactly the same phenomenon. The office space was occupied by as many young men as women. When I asked why men had been recruited, I got precisely the same answer the young people in Afghanistan had given me — that men and women need to work together to defeat oppression. Wise words.

THE TRULY INCREDIBLE PART of these reports about rape — date rape like Erica's, wartime rape such as Eva's, or the Yazidi women's ordeal with genocidal rape from the monstrous ISIS — is that this treatment of women is ubiquitous; it cuts across cultures, socioeconomic status, age, and geography. These are issues we have known about and buried forever; now they're in the spotlight. One place that spotlight blazed a hot, revealing light was in Times Square, New York City.

On a cloudy day in February 2016, in Times Square, a bride in a strapless floor-length tulle wedding gown and a veil draped over her long blond hair and around her face poses for a photograph with her husband, who is wearing a tuxedo. She's twelve. He's sixty-five. The face of the child is expressionless, the man's comfortable, even proud. A crowd gathers. People begin to ask questions. One woman moves in close to the girl and says, "Where's your mom?" Another onlooker asks the man, "How old are you? What are you doing with someone her age?" As the photographer moves them to different locations, New Yorkers do what New Yorkers do — they get involved, they press for answers. "Is she okay?" one asks. "Do you want to do this?" another inquires. One calls the groom "a fucking sick pervert." Another takes the girl's arm and gently steers her away from the man, who protests that her parents have given them their consent.

Coby Persin, a young YouTube star, set up the

shoot as a social experiment (the groom and bride were actors) after learning about child marriage not only worldwide but in the U.S. — an estimated 248,000 children as young as twelve were married in eighteen different states between 2000 and 2010. As of October 2018, eighteen U.S. states have no minimum age requirement for marriage. In two states, the minimum age is fourteen; in five states, fifteen is the minimum age; and in nineteen states, sixteen is the cut-off. The rest have a legal marriage age of eighteen, except Nebraska (nineteen) and Mississippi (twenty-one). In forty-eight states, child marriage is legal because of exceptions that allow minors to get married with parental consent or judicial approval.

In Florida, 16,400 children, some as young as thirteen, were married from 2000 to 2017 — the second-highest incidence of child marriage after Texas. In Texas from 2000 to 2014, almost forty thousand children were married. The other states with the highest known rates of child marriage are Idaho, Kentucky, Arkansas, Wyoming, Utah, Alabama, Mississippi, Texas, West Virginia, Tennessee, Missouri, Alaska, Louisiana, and South Carolina. Unchained At Last, an organization that tracks child marriage in the United States, found that in more than four hundred cases, the adult was over forty. And in thirty-one cases, they were more than sixty years old. In Alabama, a seventy-four-year-old man married a fourteen-year-old girl, though the state has since raised the minimum age of marriage to sixteen. What's more, these child brides can't run away — they cannot leave their spouse or seek shelter from abuse, because they are minors.

Around the globe, twenty-three girls under the age of sixteen are married off every minute. The highest child marriage rate in the world is in Niger, where 76 percent of girls are married before age sixteen. In Canada and in the U.K., the minimum age for marriage is sixteen. In Sudan it's ten. The Islamic Republic of Iran prohibits marriage before the "age of majority" — fifteen lunar years for boys and nine lunar years (eight years, nine months) for girls.

Invariably culture is used to justify the unacceptable against women and girls. I would give a lot to be the journalist who sits down with a sixty-year-old man on the evening of his wedding to a ten-year-old girl and ask him what the heck he thinks he's doing. I want to know how an adult condones behaviour that is perverted, grotesque,

and in fact life-threatening — and in many countries around the world, including the U.S., legal!
He would no doubt tell me it's about his religion.
I would reply that there isn't a phrase in any holy
book that says a child should be wedded to an adult.
He would then play the culture card to dismiss my
inquiry. As Farida Shaheed, the UN special rapporteur for cultural rights from 2009 to 2012, says, "If
it's your culture that allows this abuse, then change
your culture." Violence against women is always
justified in the name of culture, she says. "Whether
the culture is translated into laws such as the
personal status laws in Egypt or is part of the system — the presumed and approved behaviour of the
tribe, this is always the excuse and it is not acceptable." She calls for women to demand the cultural
rights set out in the UN's International Covenant
on Economic, Social and Cultural Rights, which
says, "All peoples have the right of self-determina-
tion. By virtue of that right, they freely determine
their political status and freely pursue their economic, social and cultural development." She hopes
women will shift their thinking from "Because of
my culture, I can't go to school or work, or decide
when to marry" to "I can decide for myself because
of my cultural rights."

Marrying a child is about sex and ownership. Every day, thirty-three thousand children are married off to adult men. The spectacle is mind-boggling: In India, a child stands solemn-faced while her mother and aunties adorn her — with a heavy gown encrusted with glitter, with henna on her tiny hands, with thick black kohl eye- and brow-liner making her little-girl eyes more prominent, with garish lipstick and a headdress so large and cumbersome it seems to weigh the child down. The family then walk this innocent child to the temple, where her future husband awaits. She's ten years old. He's sixty.

Heather Barr, acting co-director of the Women's Rights Division at Human Rights Watch, says, "Afghanistan has a tougher law on child marriage than Florida does. In Afghanistan girls can marry at 16, or at 15 with permission from their father or a judge. In Florida, a pregnant girl can marry at any age, with the approval of a judge." However, many girls marry at tender ages such as ten and twelve and thirteen in Afghanistan because of tribal law rather than state law. To allow girls to give up their childhood, to be married off as children and be basically raped by older men, is not a private family matter; it is a public health crime that needs to be exposed. These frightened little girls are used as slaves in the kitchen and the laundry room and subjected to sexual abuse and child-bearing, which often results in catastrophic health problems for the underdeveloped, too-young mother. What was once dismissed as cultural is now appropriately named criminal.

There are many ways women and girls and their sexuality can be dismissed or overlooked. It's like the anthropological and archaeological research on the history of men and women — if you aren't looking for a woman, you aren't going to find her. The same can be said in regards to the 2018 award-winning *Globe and Mail* series "Unfounded," by Robyn Doolittle. If the police aren't laying charges against the rapist, the rapist has impunity and he will reoffend and the statistics on rape will continue to go up.

The floodlight exposing the truth around the use and abuse of women's bodies has created an enveloping glare today. Margaret Atwood's *The Handmaid's Tale* is a splendid example. It was thirty years ago that she wrote the dystopian novel about the subjugation of women by forced reproduction, and yet the television series is now in season three; its second-season premiere was the Hulu network's most-watched episode of 2018. Why? Well, apart from the brilliant writing and the cleverly conceived plot, the novel is based on the notion that the Americans elect a crackpot for a president and the country is run by the religious right. Which is so close to the scenario in the U.S. today, the series could be seen as a cautionary tale.

There is evidence galore to prove that women's sexual rights have been marginalized and dismissed. Consider the judges at Nuremberg, who didn't want bawling women in their courtrooms, so women who had been sexually assaulted in the concentration camps during the Holocaust could not be heard. And it's true that when women in Herat, Afghanistan, marched in protest against Taliban rule, they were surrounded by Taliban, who apprehended the leader, soaked her with kerosene, and set her on fire. Boko Haram like to think of themselves as a religious militia saving Nigeria from a government they oppose. They are in fact bands of illiterate thugs who rape schoolgirls.

ONE THING WE DO know is that sex sells. It's a marketing tool that's made billions for many, from beer companies to car manufacturers. Sport gets the gold medal for merchandizing women's bodies. For example, when the Australian women's soccer team, quaintly called the Matildas, waltzed onto the playing field at the 2000 Sydney Olympic Games, the men in the crowd were cheering for more than victory. The women had created a sensation by posing with full frontal nudity for a pin-up calendar.

Not to be outdone by their athletic sisters, the women's rowing team in New Zealand followed suit by doffing their clothes for a calendar that showcased their well-toned, trim bodies. Unlike the Aussies, they used their paddles for a strategically placed cover-up. And across the water in the U.S. that same year, high-jump sensation Amy Acuff, whose fur-trimmed competition costumes made her look more like Bamm-Bamm in *The Flintstones* than a world-class jumper, took a page out of the same book when she did her own calendar photo in nothing but a pair of stockings and an American flag painted on each breast.

Those nearly naked athletic Olympic bodies were seeking another kind of gold — cold, hard cash from sponsors. The way to sponsorship heaven for women athletes was mega-marketing and sex. Feminists were furious. Advertisers were drooling. The athletes were enthusiastic. The International

Olympic Committee was wringing its hands. What to do? Let the games begin.

Beach volleyball, for example, fought for the right to play in the Olympic Games, but when it finally became an authorized Olympic sport at the Atlanta Games in 1996, its rules made it seem like the babe category of competition. The women's pairs were required to wear the itsiest of itsy-bitsy bikinis: no back, low front, high-cut legs, maximum six centimetres of fabric at the hip.

Sexualizing women athletes isn't new. The late Florence Griffith Joyner from the U.S. was known as much for her long, painted nails and sexy running gear as for her extraordinary athleticism. German figure skater Katarina Witt, who was chastised for her too-short skating skirt at the Calgary Olympics in 1988 and then posed nude for *Playboy* magazine, had double billing as a skater with both incredible strength and style. But the calendar pin-ups, coupled with the controversial rulings of the Fédération Internationale de Volleyball (FIVB), sparked a raging debate in athletic circles in 2000. "Are we selling sports and athleticism or sex and bodies?" asked Canadian beach volleyball player Kristine Drakich. The answer is as plain as the TV remote, according to Toronto-based writer David

Menzies, who was covering marketing trends for Sun News at the time and later moved to the Rebel, a Canadian version of Breitbart News: "Would a raving heterosexual like me pause while channel surfing for more than a nano-second to watch volleyball? Trust me, the appeal of the beach version has little to do with watching volleyball in the great outdoors and a whole lot to do with observing some beautiful, nicely toned athletes working up a sweat in revealing swimwear. I'd argue that scantily clad females fighting it out on the beach helps the sponsor and the game too."

That's the kind of retro thinking the FIVB was counting on and marketers were looking for at the time, since the primary demographic for sports-viewing fans is eighteen-to-thirty-four-year-old males. Although the viewing audience was stunned by the dynamics and fitness the sport requires, and the athleticism attached to it, the debate in Sydney fuelled a controversy all the way to the medal podium. The FIVB rules stated that the women players had to wear their playing suits (the sexy low-cut togs) on the podium for medal presentations. The men, on the other hand, could wear the tracksuit uniforms their countries provided.

The path to the podium has been hard-fought

for women. The dualities are indeed perplexing. Synchronized swimming, for example, has to be the most demanding of athletic pursuits. It began in early twentieth century as an offshoot of water ballet, was glamorized by Esther Williams in Hollywood, and became an Olympic event in 1984. So why the pancake makeup, the glitter, the Madame Tussaud garishness, in a sport that requires an almost superhuman combination of grace and power?

The thing is, sex does sell, like hotcakes. The Matildas' soccer pin-up calendar was a huge hit, selling nearly forty thousand copies. More to the point, their sport, which wasn't even on the radar screen, is now a major draw. The Olympic Games has always had a guileful take on women. In the late 1940s and '50s, every little girl in Canada wanted a skirt that twirled like Barbara Ann Scott's when they skated on the backyard pond. The film *A League of Their Own*, starring Madonna and Geena Davis, depicts another example of successful marketing in the forties. Dr. Helen Lenskyj, a retired professor of sociology at the University of Toronto, says, "When the All-American Girls Baseball League started, the theory was the American boys were off to war, and morale needed to be kept up at home, so the women were asked to step in. But Wrigley [the sponsor] had to make sure the women weren't mannish, or the idea wouldn't sell. So the girls had to wear skirts short enough that their bloomers were showing when they slid into the bases."

The good news today is that, like many other women, the athletes themselves made a winning case for change. The cold weather at the Sydney Olympics started the trend by establishing a need for the women athletes to cover up to stay warm, but it was the push to increase the number of countries competing in the Olympics that meant uniforms had to evolve for cultural and religious reasons. When Misty May-Treanor and Kerri Walsh Jennings won gold for the U.S. in beach volleyball in 2004, 2008, and again in 2012, they wore whatever suited them for competition. So did the 2016 winners from Germany, Laura Ludwig and Kira Walkenhorst. The Olympics have done a 360-degree turnaround since the late nineties when it comes to women champions. Pounding down the track, diving to hit a volleyball that's two inches away from the sand, soaring over a high-jump bar, or powering through the water is the Olympian's quest. They seek higher, faster, stronger, not erotica.

FROM CHASTITY BELTS TO breast reduction, women have travelled a distance to reach the elusive finish line for equality. Step by ever-tenacious and ever-hopeful step, they are taking action and making bold changes. For example, when Canadian member of parliament Margaret Mitchell presented the idea of a sweeping reform of the judiciary to the House of Commons in 1982 — reform that included criminalizing marital rape and making sexual assault, including wife abuse, child abuse, and incest, a crime — her fellow members of parliament laughed! They actually called to each other across the floor of the House of Commons: "I don't beat my wife. Do you, George?" Ha, ha, ha. When the new sexual assault bill passed in 1983, nobody was laughing. Those changes are being demanded elsewhere in the world today, and the conversations women are having are life-altering. At the Olympics, in the bedroom, and even in places like China and India, where the infanticide of baby girls resulted in a shortage of brides for eighty million additional men, the changemakers are altering policies, making draconian acts into headlines, and calling on human rights institutions to right the wrongs for women and girls.

The Bosnian women made rape a war crime.

Pat Barker took back the night for Homer's women. Even the Olympians said, "Keep your rules off my playbook." And women the world over busted the taboos in talking about child marriage, date rape, and the violence women have forever known. It brings to mind the famous proverb based on a line by the Greek poet Dinos Christianopolous: they thought they could bury us; they didn't know we were seeds.

CHAPTER THREE

A HOLY PARADOX

ON A SCALE OF ONE TO TEN, religion and custom concerning women and girls score a solid eleven for toxic mix. The good news is that the disruption that's prevalent everywhere in the world today is also forcing a new accounting of the holy orders and the cultural contradictions that have prevailed for centuries. The dismissive and silencing comment "Because that's the way we do things" no longer carries the clout it once did.

Today, ancient rituals and customary habits are being challenged by women who gather the information they need, make a case for change, and move ahead on intractable files such as female genital mutilation, polygamy, honour killing, and sexual abuse by Catholic priests. Adding fuel to the fire is the discovery of forgotten women whose lives have been marking the way forward since the dawn of civilization. In this chapter we'll meet some of them — a nameless nun whose blue teeth busted a long-held myth about women, and an iconic nun who defied the clerics and claimed that sexual pleasure was not a sin and should not be associated with guilt. We'll meet a group of girls in Kenya who made history when they sued their government for failing to protect them from being raped, and the splendid women of Malicounda Bambara in Senegal who were the first to eradicate female genital mutilation. And we'll hear from the woman who said freedom of religion does not allow a man to have 27 wives and 149 children, and from a brave young woman in Canada who brought truth from the Quran to the twenty-first century. These doctrines and customs have roots in history that was written mostly about men and by men, and they come from religious texts created by apostles like St. Paul, and speeches from scholars like Aristotle. Mostly they are beliefs that perpetuate themselves simply because they were not questioned. Now history needs to balance the past by adding the chronicles of women who have been seeking change throughout the millennia. Let's start with the nun with blue teeth.

WHEN THE BURIED FACTS of her life were first recorded, she was simply skeleton B78, found in an unmarked grave in 1989 in Dalheim, Germany, where an industrialist was digging up a plot of land to build a new structure. There in the dig was a cemetery. The law dictated that bodies and their graves needed to be preserved, so they were. Because the cemetery was so deep in the ground, it became obvious that there was more to the plot of land than an old burial ground. Further excavation between 1989 and 1991 unearthed a monastery. That's when the exhumed B78 was taken to a lab for analysis and radiocarbon dating.

As it turns out, skeleton B78 was about a thousand years old, a woman, and likely a nun. She was probably between the ages of forty-five and sixty when she died between 997 and 1162. And she seemed to have blue teeth. The forensic examiner presumed it was azurite causing a blue tinting of the tartar, or calculus, on her teeth. The nameless nun was stored away.

Ms. B78 spent twenty years in storage. Her

story surfaced once in a while when anthropologists questioned oddities such as blue teeth;
meanwhile, the lives of women became a topic of
increasing interest to researchers of archaeology
and anthropology. In 2011, a calculus expert, Anita
Radini at York University in England, heard the
story about the nun with blue teeth and decided to
have a look. That's when the facts of Skelton B78's
life began to come into focus. What Radini's eagle
eye caught were little specks, like miniature robin's
eggs, buried in her teeth. And that set off a series
of experiments and studies that would alter what
we know about the lives of women at the time.

Radini, who is the co-first author of the study,
knew she was onto something big but didn't know
how big when she began her work. A lot of information can be gathered from calculus — what people
ate, what textile fabrics they wore (they tend to get
caught in our teeth), DNA, bacteria. The positioning of
the blue particles in the calculus suggested that they
were absorbed at different times during this woman's
life. Radini looked for plant micro-fossils — pollen,
starch granules, and phytoliths — and found plenty
of those, but none of them explained the blue pigment. She tested a piece of the mysterious blue specks
in a dish of acid — it dissolved! The methods of

unravelling the mysterious past have been improving in leaps and bounds in the last decade, which is why, for example, handprints in caves can identify the age and sex of the artist. In this case, the methods for testing calculus that's a thousand years old were being changed and improved. But what was the blue substance? And why did this woman, long dead, have it embedded in her teeth? The collected data turned into an anthropological investigation with all the intrigue of a whodunnit.

Using micro-Raman spectroscopy, scientists from a dozen universities across eight countries, including Canada and the U.S., further analyzed the blue flecks, eventually discovering that they were lapis lazuli in a powdered form called ultramarine. It could only have come from faraway Afghanistan, and in fact, at that time in history, it was the rarest and most valuable pigment in the world, more precious than gold.

So how did a middle-aged woman, who according to an osteological investigation had lived a fairly soft life (had not done physical labour) and was buried in a cemetery next to a women's religious community, have a rare and valuable pigment in her teeth?

The researchers knew that the nearby church

and the monastery next to it were lost in a fire during one of the battles fought in the area during the fourteenth century. They also knew that only highly skilled scribes and artists had access to luxurious materials such as gold and, in some rare cases, for the truly exceptional scribes, ultramarine for writing the holy scriptures and the books of the day. It is also a fact that before the fifteenth century, scribes didn't sign their work. It was always presumed that monks were the authors of the books produced during the Middle Ages. Although it was accepted as fact that only monks were literate, the best books preserved from that time were found in women's monasteries or the remains of religious women's shelters. No one ever questioned why the books were stored in convents for women.

Many theories were advanced about the blue teeth of the exhumed nun, but only one made sense. "Based on the distribution of the pigment in her mouth, we concluded that the most likely scenario was that she was herself painting with the pigment and licking the end of the brush while painting," says co-first author Monica Tromp of the Max Planck Institute for the Science of Human History in Jena, Germany. Skeleton B78 was a scribe — a bona fide female scribe.

The work the anthropologists and archaeologists did in establishing these facts provides proof of long-distance trading routes and commercial business between far-flung countries as early as the eleventh century. It also establishes the historical value of women's monasteries and their role in book production. Women were not only literate, they were prolific creators and consumers of books.

"Here we have direct evidence of a woman, not just painting, but painting with a very rare and expensive pigment, and at a very out-of-the way place," says Christina Warinner of the Planck Institute and the senior author of the work on B78. "This woman's story could have remained hidden forever without the use of these techniques [micro-Raman spectroscopy]. It makes me wonder how many other artists we might find in medieval cemeteries — if we only look." And later, in an email to me, she said: "I do think the study alters how anthropologists consider gender in the past. Most importantly, I hope this approach will be taken up by others to examine the gender dimensions of craft activities, art, and professions in the past."

I asked her why it took so long from excavation in 1989 to publication in 2019. Here's what she said: "The lapis lazuli finding was an unexpected surprise, and it took us a while to build the right team for the analysis. It isn't usual for a study to take so long, but in this case it did because we originally had a very different focus and this [lapis lazuli] was a side finding. For a long time we thought it was just a common blue pigment like azurite, so it was a kind of back burner project. But then once the first elemental results came back as lapis lazuli, that changed everything. All of us initially involved in the project were working on several other projects at the time, and none of us had expertise in mineral analysis. It took us a while to figure out what methods existed and which were appropriate, and to build up a good team of physicists and historians. Once we started working on it in earnest, it took about 1.5 years to publication, which is about a typical project period."

Skeleton B78 wasn't the only woman who was contributing intellectually and socially almost a thousand years ago. Hildegard von Bingen was a German Benedictine abbess and, more than that, an outspoken feminist. She was also a poet, philosopher, theologian, singer, composer, playwright, artist, architect, biographer, doctor, botanist, herbalist, visionary, preacher, seer, prophet, and finally saint. Here is a woman who is credited by musicologists with inventing opera and who encouraged nuns to drink beer, which she said was safer than their drinking water and made them rosier. She even created a *lingua ignota* ("unknown language"). Born in Rhineland in 1098, she was sent to live with the nuns in a convent when she was only eight years old. She took her religious vows in her teens and became mother superior at age thirty-eight. She claimed she had visions. In fact, she claimed God wanted her to make those visions public. Not everyone in her diocese agreed. A power struggle ensued, and in 1150 she packed up and moved to Rupertsberg, near Bingen, and founded a new abbey with the fifty nuns who followed her.

She ran her abbey like a modern-day spa, promoting reading, theology, warm baths, regular exercise, singing, and playing musical instruments. And she called herself a doctor: according to legend, such large crowds gathered for her miraculous healings that her fellow nuns lobbied the bishop to order her to stop performing them.

She wrote plays, poetry, operas, and medical books. Although it was forbidden for women to preach, she went on four preaching tours, each of which lasted several years. And she got away with defying the laws of the land because the pope saw her as a seer.

When she was eighty, Hildegard committed what was probably her most audacious act. She buried a revolutionary in a grave beside her abbey. When ordered to exhume the body, she fought back, claiming she had heard the man's confession and had absolved him of his sins, thereby allowing him to be buried in the cemetery. The clerics said they would dig up the body themselves, so she quickly removed all the tombstones.

Her beliefs established her fame. She rejected the church's view of women as subservient to men and defied sexist stereotypes of the evil seductress, and she taught that woman was indeed created in the image and likeness of God. She claimed that God's inner being contains an near-erotic mingling of feminine and masculine elements, and that complementary male/female relations mirror that divine balance. She took on the teachings of St. Paul, asserting that man and woman were created for each other; woman had not been made merely for man. In opposition to St. Augustine's doctrine, she insisted that sexual pleasure is not sinful and existed in Eden before the Fall. And she had particular views about Eve, who she believed was more the devil's victim than the corrupter of Adam. She even argued that menstruation does not render a woman unclean, but bloodshed in battle does render a soldier unclean.

In 1940, the Vatican made her a saint. Recognized today as a strong feminist leader, Hildegard was named a doctor of the church. She is one of only four women on whom the revered title has ever been bestowed. Until 1970, no woman had been named a doctor of the church, but since then, four additions to the list have been women: Saints Teresa of Ávila and Catherine of Siena, by Pope Paul vi; Thérèse de Lisieux, by John Paul ii; and Hildegard, by Benedict xvi.

Hildegard and the unnamed nun with the blue teeth lived at a time when dogma relegated women to minor and subservient roles. It was Aristotle who said, "The female is female by virtue of a certain lack of qualities. We should regard women's nature as suffering from natural defectiveness." Augustine of Hippo, who would become St. Augustine, said, "What is the difference whether it is in a wife or a mother; it is still Eve, the temptress that we must beware of in any woman. I fail to see what use woman can be to man, if one excludes the function of bearing children." Despite the egalitarian preaching of nuns like Hildegard, and even the new evidence that a thousand years ago women had greater status than was believed, it's only recently that such rhetoric has been exposed as misogyny. Shedding this nonsense has been a gargantuan task, something akin to miracles.

It all goes back to the earliest religious texts. The Book of Genesis describes the creation of the first woman this way: "And the rib, which the Lord God had taken from man, made he a woman, and brought her to the man. And Adam said, 'This is now bone of my bone, and flesh of my flesh: she shall be called Woman, because she was taken out of Man'" (2:22–23).

There are people alive today who actually believe this. In fact, the Yazidi people — who in 2014 suffered what they call their seventy-fourth genocide and in particular made world headlines because more than five thousand Yazidi women and girls were captured and held as sex slaves by ISIS — told me a version of this Adam and Eve story in 2017. The truth for the Yazidis lies in a place called Lalish, their spiritual home. They like to say this place, about a twenty-minute drive west of Duhok in Northern Iraq, is as old as the world and is the actual Garden of Eden. A winding road leads up to the temple, which sits on acres of property with gnarled trees and twisted hanging vines covering old stone cell-like buildings that are protected by rolling mountains on three sides. Even on a winter day with leafless trees and unexpected snow, the ambiance evokes yesteryear. The huge temple with its ancient anterooms — where one must go barefoot on old stone floors worn to a shiny white finish, even on the day I visit during a snowstorm — has the rarified air of a holy place.

The Yazidis claim to be the oldest people on earth, direct descendants of Adam but not Eve, as according to their teachings, her reproductive seed was impure. The Yazidis believe that Adam's son, Shehid bin Jer, was incubated in a vessel containing his father's seed. It's an extraordinary story told by people who have suffered horribly at the hands of barbarians. But like so many negatives in theology, the story paints women as the devil, making it hard for me to accept.

Misogynists invariably claim they act in the name of God. The Old Testament, written between 1200 and 165 BCE, was the original religious document for Christians, Jews, and Muslims — Judaism came first, in about 900 BCE; then, about a thousand years later, Christianity made its mark, followed in 600 CE by Islam. And it contains damning verses about women. The Apocryphal book of Ecclesiasticus, in a passage about head-strong daughters, says: "Keep a strict watch on her shameless eye; do not be surprised if she disgraces you" (26:11).

But the New Testament sealed the social destiny of women in Christianity. The sentiment "Wives, submit yourselves unto your own husbands, as it is fit in the Lord" is repeated three times in three different books (Colossians 3:18, 1 Peter 3:1, and Ephesians 5:22). Paul's letter to the Corinthians says, "Women should remain silent in the churches. They are not allowed to speak, but must be in submission, as the law says. If they want to inquire about something, they should ask their own husbands at home; for it is disgraceful for a woman to speak in the church" (1 Corinthians 14:34–35). (In fairness to St. Paul, there have been ongoing — make that never-ending — discussions about how he could have written that passage and others equally hurtful to women; some conclude that his letter was rewritten by a later author. If that's the case, why does the passage remain in print?) And this is from 1 Timothy 2:12: "I permit no woman to teach or have authority over a man; she is to keep silent."

The Quran and Torah have similarly discrim-
inatory injunctions against women inheriting or
owning property. The tone is also noteworthy. The
rabbinical commentary to Sanhedrin 71a:8 states:
"With regard to his mother, from where does she
have independently owned property that her son
can steal? The basis for this question is the *halakha*
that anything that a woman acquires is acquired
by her husband."

The Quran was delivered by God through the
archangel Gabriel to the Prophet Muhammad over
twenty-three years, from 609 to 632. It promoted
women's rights in marriage, divorce, and inheritance.
It also prohibited female infanticide and recognized
women as full persons. But the Quran also belittles
women, as in Al-Baqarah 228: "Men have a status
above women. Allah is mighty and wise."

Equally offensive remarks have been made by
so-called holy people right up to and including
today. In 1992, seeking to rally opposition to a proposed Iowa equal rights amendment, the former
Southern Baptist leader Pat Robertson wrote, in
a fundraising letter to supporters of the Christian
Coalition, that the "feminist agenda" is "not about
equal rights for women"; instead, he said, "it is
about a socialist, anti-family political movement

that encourages women to leave their husbands, kill their children, practice witchcraft, destroy capitalism and become lesbians."

Fifteen hundred years ago, the Prophet Muhammad was married to a businesswoman. Nine hundred years ago in Baghdad, the home of Islam, women owned businesses. Some were doctors. At the time, Islam was the only religion that tolerated practice of another religion. So why do so many leaders today interpret the Quran oppressively, allowing women to be beaten, claiming that their word is worth half of a man's in court, insisting fathers are the only legal guardians of children? The Quran was dictated directly to Muhammad, but long after the death of the Prophet, its Hadith (interpretations of the Prophet's words) was added; they tell us more about the age in which they were written than they do about the Prophet himself.

TOO OFTEN IN HISTORY, women who have been raped have been condemned as social outcasts. But modern-day women have another narrative to tell. From 2012 to 2018, I covered an astonishing story about 160 girls between the ages of three and seventeen in Meru, Kenya, who sued the government for failing to protect them from being raped. A little girl who has been raped — by her father, her uncle, her brother, neighbour, teacher, or priest — pays a lifelong price. She is not only hurt and likely sick, but she bears the awful stigma prevalent in Africa, where rape is referred to as "defilement." She can't go to school. Her health is jeopardized. She has no money and no support.

Human rights lawyers from Nairobi — all women — contacted Canadian women human rights lawyers in Canada who had successfully sued the Toronto police concerning the investigation of a predator who came to be known as the Balcony Rapist. In the 1980s, a serial rapist was operating in a Toronto neighbourhood, entering the apartments of young women from their balconies. The police figured out his modus operandi and set a trap for him. After he entered the apartment of a woman now known as Jane Doe, they caught and arrested him. Jane Doe sued the police for using her as bait without her knowledge. Police had also failed to warn women that there was a serial rapist in the neighbourhood. She won the case, setting a legal precedent.

Lawyer Fiona Sampson, who runs a non-government organization called the Equality Effect, offered guidance and assistance to the Kenyan lawyers, which turned into a three-year odyssey. When the girls won the case, they won it for ten million girls in Kenya. They wanted the other girls to know why they sued the government. They wanted to set up a nationwide educational program using drama, singing, dancing, debating clubs, and collaboration with the community and the police. Delaine Hampton, adjunct professor and executive in residence at the Rotman School of Management at the University of Toronto, handed the task to her MBA class and put them in touch with the girls.

In addition, it was decided that the judiciary, and in particular the police, would receive special training on the laws against child rape, and the enforcement of those laws. But who would take on such a huge task? They needed volunteers who were experienced, sensitive professionals. Over three years, the Sex Crimes Unit of the Vancouver Police Department volunteered with a train-the-trainer program. In March 2019 they were ready to turn over the training program to the officers in Kenya. That same day, the girls launched Justice Clubs for boys and girls in nine pilot schools across the country. Students would have a chance to discuss justice, rights, and the consequences of rape. The founders of the Justice Clubs, the 160 girls who fought the case, have been on a very long journey. They are victims, of course. But they are also enormously empowered by the action they took. They did what their big sisters didn't dare to do; they went where their mothers and aunties and grannies didn't dare to go. They became their own agents of change.

Fifteen years earlier, women in Senegal took a similarly brave step and became the first to eradicate female genital mutilation (FGM). Their courageous story came back to me in February 2019, when I received an email from Terres des Femmes in Berlin requesting a donation to support a safe house in Sierra Leone where girls could go to escape FGM. I was stunned by the casual use of the word "mutilation." When FGM became an issue in the 1980s, cultural relativists objected to the use of harsh words like "mutilation," which they argued imposed our own cultural values on other people; these women, they argued, were honouring their ancient customs. Many reporters and researchers were cowed into censorship. But there was little discussion among the cultural relativists about what actually happened to these women. Usually at the age of five but as late as adulthood, they were tied to chairs, their legs were splayed apart, and their external genitalia were sliced off with a razor blade. If they didn't bleed to death or die of septic shock, they grew up to suffer horrendous health issues: urinary tract infections, because it takes fifteen minutes to urinate with scarred genitalia, so girls and women would wait until they had enough time (and the waiting leads to a buildup of bacteria); three or four days of hard labour to deliver a child, often losing the first child because of prolonged labour. One woman in Senegal told me, "The first one always dies — that baby is preparing the way for the others." What they didn't know is that other women in other places — even in other tribes in their own countries — didn't support this old custom.

Words matter. In French-speaking Senegal, FGM is called *"excision"* — cutting. We have always found ways to soften the harshness of what we do. In Sarajevo, genocide was referred to as "ethnic cleansing." In war zones, when bombs mistakenly strike the innocent, we call it "collateral damage." In North America, we used to speak of "crimes of passion"; now we call it murder when a man kills his intimate partner. In the Middle East, it's still called "honour killing." But FGM is being called what it is today. And by all accounts, the blunt and accusatory references are working. Female circumcision has been illegal in Canada since 1997, but it is still practised secretly or during what's called "vacation cutting," when a child is sent to another country for the procedure, to avoid the consequences at home. The law here says anyone who does it, assists with it in any way, or even acts as an observer is guilty. In the U.S. as of July 2019, thirty-two states had made FGM illegal, and since 1996, federal legislation has protected girls under the age of eighteen.

Today the World Health Organization (WHO) uses the term "female genital mutilation" and has determined that the practice is rooted in gender inequality as an attempt to control a woman's sexuality. The international agencies, such as UNICEF, WHO, and Plan International, that monitor women's health agree that FGM intentionally causes injury for non-medical reasons and that it's a violation of the human rights of women and girls. Today, more than 200 million girls and women in thirty countries in North, West, and East Africa, as well as the Middle East and Asia, have undergone circumcision. But the numbers are plummeting. In East Africa, 71.4 percent of girls and women were being circumcised in 1995 compared to 8 percent in 2016. In North Africa, the number has dropped from 57.7 percent in 1990 to 14.1 percent in 2015, and in West Africa from 73.6 percent in 1996 to 25.4 percent in 2017.

The email brought back memories of my assignments in 1997 and 2004 to the village of Malicounda Bambara in Senegal. The first woman I met was Molly Melching, whom I came to think of as "unsinkable Molly." She had come to Senegal in 1974 from Danville, Illinois, on a six-month exchange program at the University of Dakar, and never left. In 1991, she started her own non-government organization called Tostan, which means "breakthrough" in the Wolof language spoken by the women in Malicounda. Molly Melching is one of those people who have so much presence, she could be standing in a doorway yet seem to be the centre of the room. She was a hero to the women who flocked to the courses she taught in health, literacy, and human rights. Melching knew all about the consequences FGM had on the health of these women, often from when they were little girls. But she also knew that to bring up the custom could create a barrier between her and the women.

One day during a literacy class, the word "cutting" came up. Molly decided to take a chance and said, "Shall we talk about it?" The women replied in one voice, "We can talk, but we will never ever change it." Then one of the group, who was a mid-wife and delivered babies in other villages, said she had noticed that women from other tribes were not circumcised. She asked the group, "Do we know why we do it?" They presumed the practice must be part of their religion and decided to ask for a meet-ing with their imam. They asked Molly about child labour and delivery, about urinating, about a host of other problems that had plagued them. They also began calculating the cost — a large portion of their hard-earned shillings from working in the fields was being spent on doctors.

I remember the quiet courage of these women. They built a one-room meeting house and painted it yellow. It was in that space that they spoke for the first time about the ritual they had gone through, the same ritual their mothers and grandmoth-ers had gone through. This was the space where a centuries-old silence was broken. Most of the women had questioned the procedure, but none dared to voice her concerns. After all, how could it be wrong if the village leaders, the imams, and the mothers and daughters who came before them had accepted this ritual as a rite of passage to becoming a proud Amazon woman, as they like to call themselves? They worried about what would happen if they didn't have their daughters circumcised. Would the decision insult their mothers and aunties and grandmothers? They knew that anyone in the village who was not circumcised was not allowed to eat with the others, go to school with the others, wash with the others. It was a frightening step to take and would surely result in consequences.

The women made a plan: they would discuss the ban with their religious leader, and together they would confront the community. The imam, who presumed FGM was a religious custom, found out there was nothing in their holy book to support that notion. He wondered if it was a cultural tradition and went to the village chief with his own questions. To the surprise of both the imam and the chief, there was no cultural expectation that involved FGM. Eventually the women stood together at a public ceremony and vowed, "Never again, not my daughter." Within two weeks, sixty more villages followed, and by year's end, half the villages in Senegal had banned the practice.

Customary procedures that harm women and girls are slowly but surely being eliminated. Foot binding in China went on for more than a thousand years. Little girls with perfectly healthy feet had their big toes turned under and their arch broken and taped so that they would have tiny, presumably delicate feet. Although many postulate that the custom was meant to stop women from running away, or even arose from a fetish men had about tiny feet, the truth is no one knows why it began. Diplomats and visiting health experts had tried to convince the Chinese of its unhealthy and debilitating consequences, but it persisted until the turn of the twentieth century, when a group of women formed a club called the Healthy Foot Society. They decided that foot binding had to end and made a public pledge: "I will never bind my daughter's feet and I will never allow my son to marry a girl whose feet have been bound." Foot binding ended almost universally in less than a dozen years. Dr. Gerry Mackie, a professor of political science at the University of California in San Diego, says it was the public pledge that won the day. His research on both foot binding and FGM shows that breaking with tradition on your own will lead to being ostracized, but "vowing to stop together avoids singling out one woman and her family."

THERE IS EVIDENCE ALL over the world that women are banding together to attack and stop harmful customs and promote change in religious and cultural practices. But old customs still turn up like mould. The oldest atrocity is one that dates back to an era called Jahiliyyah, a pre-Islamic time referred to by the Prophet Muhammad as the Time of Ignorance. Infant daughters could be buried alive to prevent them from growing up to dishonour the family. Although the Prophet vowed to eradicate the practice, honour killing still goes on today. And although the practice is usually associated with Islam, it was also prevalent among Christians in ancient Rome and Greece. Daughters weren't condemned to death to protect the family's honour; they were simply considered worthless. Infanticide was legal until 374 CE.

Today, throughout the Middle East, North Africa, Pakistan, and Afghanistan, honour killing is an unholy family alliance that allows a woman to be murdered to rid the family of shame; it keeps women in fear all of their lives. Those who favour such a law claim it is about honour and shame. It is not. It is about control and abuse. There's nothing honourable about bashing your daughter over the head with a cement slab and tossing her body down a well just because she spoke to a boy on the street. This is femicide — the killing of women. A woman can be killed by her family — beaten, burned, strangled, shot, stabbed — for any reason at all: for dating the wrong man, for being raped, for refusing to submit to the will of her father and brothers. A man can easily get rid of his wife because he wants to remarry and doesn't want the burden of being besmirched by divorce. So he simply says, "I saw her with another man," and she is killed off like a cow that fails to produce milk.

Some countries legally allow honour killings; others barely punish them, if at all. According to article 340 of the Jordanian penal code, a man whose female relative is found "guilty" of committing adultery is exempt from punishment if he kills her. Article 76 of the temporary penal code permits defendants to plead "mitigating reasons" for assault. Pressure from social groups stalled a 2011 attempt by legislators to prevent honour-killing defendants from evoking article 76.

Yet those who practise honour killings invariably attempt to cover it up — she fell down the well; she was mugged in the park; she went out with criminals. If it's not against the law, why lie? In December 1999, I asked the chief coroner for the

Palestinian Authority in East Jerusalem, Dr. Jalal Aljabri, who said he sees plenty of corpses that have all the marks of honour killing, but he hardly ever sees a case in which honour killing is the official cause of death. "In our culture, everybody knows but nobody says. I get cases that say the cause of death is a firearm injury. I know inside what really happened, but what can I do? I sign the certificate and say, 'Bye-bye; that's it.'"

A cowardly response to a vile act. Dr. Aljabri is an "enlightened" Palestinian man who said he was strongly against honour killing. But the tone changed when I asked about his own family — he has five boys and three girls. What if one of his unmarried daughters got pregnant? The question left him aghast. "A girl knows she cannot be pregnant. She cannot have sexual relations. She must understand what would happen." So I asked him again, what would he have done? "I don't know," he replied. Here is a classic example of the internalization of patriarchy: the fear of shame, of being held up as an example of a failed man who cannot control his women. Even as you know it's morally wrong to kill a daughter, the pressure to conform is so great that you ignore your conscience.

In neighbouring Ramallah, Dr. Salwa Al-Najjab,

an obstetrician/gynecologist, explained that girls are taught that the hymen is the centre of the family's honour. "I was just eleven years old when my mother told me about the hymen being like a glass; if it's broken it can never hold water again. She didn't even tell me about menstruation. Just about hymens." Every day at her clinic, someone seeks information about the state of a girl's hymen. Many still believe that a woman must bleed after intercourse on her wedding night as proof of her virginity. One doctor, who didn't want to be named, said, "If I'm asked to examine a girl to check if her hymen is in place, I always say it is. Why would I say otherwise, if I know they will kill her?"

If a doctor does disclose the damning truth and if the family has financial resources, they may choose to spare the girl's life by seeking hymen repair surgery — stitching the sides of the hymen together. Dr. Al-Najjab calls this an "unethical money-making business that exploits women."

Politics are never far from the obsession with the purity of women. The political climate can alter and shift a woman's role to protect nations, for example, as it did in some countries during the Second World War, when women were encouraged to work in factories because the men had left to fight. In a study Dr. Al-Najjab and her colleagues did after the Palestinian uprisings against Israel in the late 1980s and early 1990s, they found a correlation between political power and emancipation. "During the intifada, women were seen as partners. The young women and men passed out pamphlets, threw stones, and worked on the street together. At that time, the [honour] killing of women decreased. But when there was no change in the political situation, the women went back to their houses. Now, if they're on the street, they're seen as women, not as partners, and the rate of femicide has increased."

A family's honour is tied to public "knowing" — the need to save face. If the "crime" is not disclosed, there's no pressure to take action. But if it's made public, a girl's life becomes a tool to silence the gossips and rescue the family's honour. Arab culture casts the male as the sole protector of the female, so he must have total control of her. If his protection is violated, he loses honour because, according to his relatives and friends, either he failed to protect her or he failed to bring her up correctly.

Google and Apple took the control issues a step further when they uploaded an app that allows Saudi men to monitor the movement of their

mothers, sisters, wives, and daughters. The app
sends alerts if the woman uses her passport or her
credit card or her phone. Known as Absher, the app
was developed by the Saudi Ministry of the Interior
to provide access to government services such as
passport renewals and driving licences, but it also
tracks the women, which is legal in Saudi Arabia
because the kingdom claims men are their custodians. Human Rights Watch and others, including
women in Saudi Arabia, cried foul, but in February
2019 Google and Apple announced they would not
remove the Saudi government app because it is
legal in the country where it was created.

One of the youngest countries in the world,
Saudi Arabia was founded in 1932 by the House of
Saud — a group of powerful tribal men descended
from Muhammad bin Saud, founder of the Emirate
of Diriyah in 1744, which unified many states on
the Arabian Peninsula to free them from Ottoman
rule. There were actually three stages of the Saudi
state, all of which included Wahhabism, the ultra-
conservative and fundamentalist form of Islam, as
well as plenty of infighting that led to today's Saudi
Arabia. It was the twentieth-century discovery of
vast oil reserves that transformed the country into
an economic powerhouse geopolitically positioned

between the Middle East and the oil-consuming West. Today it is an absolute monarchy, with enormous riches and long life expectancy. It also has the worst human rights record in the world and ranks 141 out of 149 countries on the Global Gender Gap Index. The laws are traditionally uncodified, and jurisprudence is managed by the personal views and often whims of men. Beheading, stoning, amputation, crucifixion, and lashing are used to punish everything from murder to witchcraft and from flirting to robbery. Homosexual acts are punished with death. An eye for an eye is still practised — the eye of the guilty surgically removed. There is no jury trial and no lawyer, and the presumption of guilt goes with torture for anyone who doesn't confess. Women and girls couldn't go to school until the 1950s or university until 1970. They have guardians — a father, husband, brother, or son who controls their every move. Without permission from a male guardian, a Saudi woman cannot apply for a passport, travel abroad, get married or divorced, open a bank account, start a business, file a police report, or get elective surgery.

The kingdom claims to have eased restrictions on women in the recent past — forced marriage became illegal in 2005; a female joined the ranks of government ministers in 2009; Saudi women were allowed to compete in the Olympic Games as of 2012 and gained the right to vote in 2015. By 2017, a Saudi woman was head of the stock exchange; in 2018 women were allowed to drive; and in 2019 a new ruling ordered that a woman must be informed by text when the court grants a divorce to her husband. Imagine that. But women still have severe restrictions on their lives. They cannot mix with men in public and must be covered in the body-enveloping abaya.

In 2018, Crown Prince Mohammed bin Salman had more than a dozen activists arrested who had campaigned for women's right to drive. The shiny new progress began to lose its sheen. Then, in October 2018, Jamal Khashoggi, an exiled Saudi journalist who worked for the *Washington Post*, was murdered and dismembered in the Saudi consulate in Turkey. In January 2019, eighteen-year-old Rahaf Mohammed al-Qunun (who has now dropped the family name al-Qunun) was granted asylum in Canada after running away from her abusive family, who she said threatened to kill her because she had cut her hair and disavowed her religion.

The guardianship system has helped create some of the most gender-unequal countries in the

Middle East. To disobey is to die. Honour killing is part of the religious code. That's the thing about unchecked religion and custom; for centuries they have been used to justify the sidelining, marginalizing, abusing, and even killing of women. One of the most hideous honour killings happened in Canada — near Kingston, Ontario — in 2009. According to the prosecution's version of how the murder unfolded, Mohammad Shafia and his second wife, Tooba Yahya, along with their son, Hamed, used one vehicle to ram another into a canal. Inside were their daughters — nineteen-year-old Zainab, seventeen-year-old Sahar, and thirteen-year-old Geeti — and Mohammad's first wife, Rona Amir, all of whom had been hit on the head and were unconscious. Mohammad, Tooba, and Hamed were found guilty of first-degree murder and sentenced to life in prison with no chance of parole for twenty-five years.

IN THE U.S. AND CANADA, a sect of the Mormon Church called the Fundamentalist Church of Jesus Christ of Latter-Day Saints (FLDS) has been using and abusing women in the name of God for a century. The timeline stretches back to 1904, when the

Mormon Church outlawed polygamy. The members of the FLDS refused to relinquish the practice, claiming it follows the teaching in the Book of Mormon that the only way for a man to survive the apocalypse is through abundant reproduction through plural marriage to the youngest, the prettiest, and the smartest women available. Today, about ten thousand followers in Utah, Arizona, Texas, Colorado, South Dakota, Alberta, and British Columbia, under the guise of freedom of religion, cling to tenets that defy both civil law and human rights law (involving underage marriage, sex with minors, trafficking in child brides as they move between Utah and British Columbia, and the collection of child tax credits on hundreds of kids).

In 1988, Debbie Palmer, who was taken into the religious sect by her parents at the age of two and married off to a fifty-five-year-old man when she was fifteen, decided to blow the whistle on all of them — the bishops, the husbands, the followers, and even the attorney general of British Columbia. She argued that the holy vows the FLDS men took "were not about sex for salvation but sex for breeding cheap labour."

In 2004, I went to Bountiful, British Columbia, to interview Debbie. She has been married three times to men with multiple wives, as a result of which she has eight children, seventy-six stepchildren, forty-seven brothers and sisters, and three ex-husbands.

"I now realize I am my own step-great-grandmother," she said.

By the time I visited, the secrets of the polygamous cult were leaking out — early warning signs of a deluge. In fact, as I drove to the gate, I could see the young girls in the distance with their long, braided hair and paisley floor-length, long-sleeved dresses. Then I noticed the round field rocks painted white and arranged in a semicircle at the gate. The woman I was driving with said those rocks used to say "Keep Sweet" — the mantra the women were told to honour. But that day someone had turned the stones over and painted "Fuck Off!!" on the other side.

It's difficult to fathom that in countries like Canada and the U.S., such partnerships in the name of God still exist. In September 2007, the FLDS president, Warren Jeffs, finally went on trial in Utah and was found guilty of sexually assault-ing his twelve- and fifteen-year-old child brides and sentenced to life in prison. But in Bountiful, the leader of the sect, Winston Blackmore, who had 24 wives and 149 children and kept a breeding chart on the wall so he knew which wife was ovulating and therefore which wife to have sex with each night, was found guilty of polygamy and given six months' house arrest and twelve months' probation.

Debbie Palmer kept her own kids and grandchildren at a safe distance from men in the FLDS, who continue to think nightly sex with young girls is ordained by God.

MOTHERS WILL GO to extraordinary lengths to protect their daughters from predatory men. In Cameroon, breast ironing made headlines when several cases turned up in Britain. This is a practice in which mothers press hot stones or spatulas onto their pubescent daughters' budding breasts to stop them from growing. The aim is to protect their daughters from being raped by men and impregnated, which would result in cutting short their education and submitting them to early marriage — 65 percent of girls who drop out of school leave because of pregnancy. Twenty-five percent of the girls in Cameroon have endured this painful procedure. One needs to ask why there are no measures taken to stop men demanding sex from young girls.

In Malawi, where 42 percent of girls are married by eighteen and 9 percent by fifteen, two women who became hereditary chiefs in two different districts shocked their tribes, as well as the government, not only by demanding an end to child marriage but furthermore by annulling marriages and sending girls back to school.

In 2013, Chalendo MacDonald, who was married herself at age fourteen, became Chief Mwanza and now presides over 760 villages and 170 village headmen, including her own husband. When she took office, she spoke publicly about the need for girls to be educated and called for better enforcement of laws against gender-based violence and a ban on child marriage, as well as the elimination of initiation rites that were harmful to girls. Her work and leadership resulted in invitations to Ethiopia and Uganda, and she has been visited by the late Nelson Mandela's wife, Graça Machel.

In another district, Senior Chief Theresa Kachindamoto took the same action when she met with her fifty sub-chiefs—she banned child marriage outright and annulled 850 marriages on the spot and sent the girls back to school. To the great surprise of most observers, including the United Nations Population Fund workers in the area, the government of Malawi voted unanimously to amend the constitution and change the law to make the legal age of marriage eighteen.

Even the pope has finally acknowledged that for decades there have been priests who sexually assaulted parishioners, some of them children, some of them nuns. The Catholic Church made headlines when a nun with the Missionaries of Jesus in the southern state of Kerala, India, accused a visiting bishop, Franco Mulakkal, of raping her. The story went viral, partly for the fact that it took almost two years for the Church to acknowledge the accusation. According to the nun, on May 4, 2014, the night before the bishop was to celebrate her nephew's First Communion, he called her to his quarters and raped her. Later she would tell the Church that he continued to rape her and other nuns in the convent in the years that followed. Her complaints to her superiors went unheeded. The hush order was more powerful than truth. In September 2017, Bishop Mulakkal was finally arrested; in April, he was charged with illegal confinement, criminal intimidation, unnatural sex, rape, and misuse of power.

As it turns out, the attack on the nun was not an uncommon assault. Police in Kerala say more nuns have come forward to accuse four priests of blackmailing women, using information shared during confession to coerce them into sex.

Reports of sexual abuse in the Catholic Church were nothing new by this point. In 2002, the *Boston Globe* uncovered a major scandal implicating the Church in a systemic cover-up of sexual abuse of minors by clergy. In 2018, a grand jury report released in Pennsylvania alleged the Church had covered up seventy years of abuse by three hundred priests; the victims numbered at least a thousand, and it was likely that thousands more remained unidentified because of lost records or fear of coming forward. The complicity in Boston and Pennsylvania as well as faraway Kerala was colossal. In 2018, Pope Francis acknowledged the widespread problem and vowed (like those before him) to take action. In the meantime, Bishop Mulakkal is out on bail, awaiting trial.

IF HISTORY EXAMINED CIVILIZATIONS by the way they treated women, it's likely we would have a different outcome for women and girls today. Every civilization from the Sumerians to the Greeks and Romans and from primitive to tribal to space-age has devised a plan and a place for women: as goddess, mother, concubine, harlot, slave; as feminist, upstart, disruptor. We have worn labels for thousands of years, but the struggle to shed the monikers and gain our right to freedoms of speech, sexuality, and movement, to control our own bodies and choose our own careers and pave our own way, has never been far beneath the surface. From Enheduanna, the Sumerian high priestess who spoke for fairness and justice for women five thousand years ago, to Christine de Pizan, who dared to raise her voice about inequality in 1400, to the nuns like Hildegard and outspoken critics like Mary Wollstonecraft, the struggle has never ceased despite the considerable influence of religion and custom.

The women of Afghanistan, whom I have been following as a journalist for more than two decades, are an example of the toxic mix of these two facets of humanity. Ancient traditions and religion have a way of complicating matters. Politics have a way of confounding them. When I met these women soon after the Taliban took over on September 26, 1996, I could hardly believe my eyes. They were the epitome of a human rights catastrophe, and yet the world was looking the other way. While burkas were already common in the rural areas of the country, now every woman had to wear one; she couldn't leave her home unless she was in the company of a husband, brother, or son; she had to wear wedge shoes because the Taliban didn't like the *tap tap tap* of a woman's heels. Television was forbidden. They were not allowed to sing or listen to music. Clapping was forbidden, as was loud laughter. The schools were closed. Unchaperoned women could seek medical help only from other women. Makeup and nail polish were banned and carried brutal punishments, including being whipped by the police of the Vice and Virtue Ministry — a collection of thugs who roamed the streets looking for women to punish. Little girls were told their dolls were un-Islamic, as the only image allowed was that of the Prophet, so they were instructed to throw their dollies into bonfires. This was at a time when we could land a man on the moon, cure many cancers, send messages via cyberspace.

The country quickly sank into the Dark Ages, and the women became a holy paradox. It didn't take long for them to start clandestine schools and health clinics. Like undercover cops, they labelled girls' schools as centres of Islamic studies but inside taught chemistry and math and literature to those who dared come to class. Women deemed un-Islamic were carted off to the soccer stadium and stoned to death in front of a crowd of cheering men, just as in the Roman coliseum with its lions and Christians two thousand years before. The women told me the Taliban would bury the woman up to her neck in a hole in the middle of the stadium and make a circle around her and throw rocks at her head until she was dead. The Taliban rule was that you could not throw a stone so big as to kill her quickly. All around me, I saw women under siege, and yet, as women always do, they would pour green tea and tell me stories about their kids and their kitchens, and they would kibitz about the craziness in their lives.

When this began in 1996, 85 percent of the women in Afghanistan were illiterate. They referred to their illiteracy as blindness. When I asked a woman to explain, she used fewer than a dozen words to describe the very root of women's oppression: "I couldn't read so I couldn't see what was going on." One of the additional problems is that the Quran is written in Arabic. Most Afghans speak either Dari or Pashto and can't read a word

of the holy book. So religious mullahs and tribal
leaders get to tell the others what they think the
Quran says and often prescribe deplorable rules
that are more about political opportunism than
religious doctrine. For example, a tribal law called
baad is used to settle disputes between tribes. The
losing tribe has to give a girl — preferably a young
girl about the age of five, or sometimes two girls,
depending on the size of the harm done — to the
vexed tribe to settle the score. What happens to
these little girls is nearly unspeakable. I once asked
a man how he could condone such wretched treatment of a child, and he said, "We know it is wrong,
but it is our way." There's no place in the Quran
that says a woman can't go to school or that she
must cover her face or that a child must be given
up as ransom. The Taliban often made up the rules
as they went along, but for five long years nobody
challenged them — until 9/11. Afterwards, the
American military and their NATO allies invaded
the country, got rid of the Taliban, and exposed
the catastrophic conditions for women. Each time
I returned, there was change — the schools were
opening, the women were back at work, the hateful
Vice and Virtue police had vanished, and the burka-
clad women were emerging from their cocoons.

For the next thirteen years, the women wrote a new future for themselves in the government as members of parliament and cabinet ministers and governors; in the universities as professors and students; in business as entrepreneurs; in the arts as designers, singers, conductors, and writers; and in sports as rugby players and extreme cyclists and hang-gliders. Then the international community left in 2014, and the Taliban, along with half a dozen other insurgencies, tested the soft underbelly of the fledgling Afghan military. While Afghans continued to go to school and work and to cope with the gridlocked traffic on the city streets, a renewed fear skirted their lives in the form of suicide bombers and rocket-propelled grenades exploding in public places. Despite the fact that Afghan men, women, and children had never been better off — life expectancy increased from forty-seven to sixty-two years; maternal mortality fell by 75 percent; polio was almost eradicated; 9.6 million students were back at school, 39 percent of them girls — people around the world thought the place was an armed camp where no one dared to go outside, and that the country was a lost cause. Then, eyeing the upcoming 2020 election, President Donald Trump realized he needed to fulfill a promise made to his supporters, a promise that he'd bring the American troops home from Afghanistan. Peace talks with the Taliban seemed to be the most expedient route to being re-elected, and the women of Afghanistan, and the elected government, were tossed under the bus.

They have banded together again, just as they did in secret meetings when the Taliban took over, to protect their hard-won rights and survive another round of the fight that barters their rights for a piece of land.

So many times women have staggered up to the barriers of change and found a way to storm through an opening. Yet ancient beliefs that baby girls are worthless, that women bring shame to the family simply because they are women, continue to infect even twenty-first-century thinking.

History tells us that those thoughts have been there, embedded in our psyches, since the dawn of civilization. But also there, embedded right beside these patriarchal thoughts, have been women's ideas of how to right the wrongs. Forcing a truth telling, finding ways to share their stories. Eventually their message about the need for change was taken up by men.

Throughout the past millennia, voices continued

to suggest that the way forward ought to include women. In the year 1000, when skeleton B78 was writing texts with the most expensive material in the world, women in France had to cover their heads, and men in Germany had the right to sell their wives. But in the world of Islam, in parts of Spain and North Africa and the Middle East to the Indus Valley, extreme restrictions on women were apparently few. In Egypt during the Fatimid reign, the House of Wisdom, an institution of higher learning, had rooms for women, and boys and girls were raised as equals. In early Sung Dynasty China, women were free of the restrictions that would arrive later that period, and they included notable warriors and writers who rank among the great heroines of Chinese history. Later, with the advent of Confucianism, came female infanticide, foot binding, and the seclusion of women.

Toward the end of that millennium, the suffrage movement began its series of successes. It was the beginning of the fall of old presumptions about women in power. However, religious doctrine prevailed, with carefully crafted messages about hearth and home — that good women wanted to be there baking pies and tending to toddlers (no mention of making financial ends meet, keeping children healthy in the face of epidemics, and handling temper tantrums and sibling rivalries — just women's work) — that women who went to work were selfish and didn't care about their husbands or their kids. But during the First World War and again during the Second World War, women picked up hoes to keep the farms going and went to work in the factories (particularly munitions factories) when the men (and a few women) left for war.

It wasn't until well into the twentieth century that women would begin to shed the shackles of religious-based laws and customary beliefs that had kept them away from professions, off juries, and out of the paid workforce. But religion continues to be a powerful force in the lives of women, and in some places it is having a resurgence. In post-Communist countries such as Croatia, Poland, and Hungary, the Catholic Church is gaining traction on conservative causes, such as denying reproductive rights and the rights of LGBTQ citizens. The Orthodox Church and followers of Islam are also leaning on old conservative values that kept women out of the workforce and tied to hearth and home. The wording of the Istanbul Convention, the first legally binding instrument aimed at preventing and combating violence against women, including physical, psychological, and domestic violence, leaves no doubt: there can be no real equality between women and men if women are the target of large-scale gender-based violence and state agencies and institutions turn a blind eye. In 2012, all the European Union countries signed the Istanbul Convention, but as of February 2019, eight member states had yet to ratify it.

"Religion has not withered away," says Farida Shaheed, former United Nations special rapporteur on cultural rights. "It is back and has increased in power, even in Eastern Europe. The issue is who does the interpretation of what religion means: religion as faith is the least problematic; as custom, it's a bigger problem; but as politics, it becomes the most problematic. Religion is being harnessed to further political agendas."

Shaheed's research around the world shows some intriguing trends. "It's often not just religious groups who use religion for power," she says. "It's used for alliances across the board of very conservative agendas." Many of those agendas are written in government offices, not in mosques.

Today, women are speaking up at home, in the village square, at the office water cooler, and in publications like never before. Sabha Sajjad-Hazai is a lawyer in Ontario. She is also a member of the national board of the Canadian Council of Muslim Women. In the winter of 2019, she decided it was time to speak her truth about polygamy within her religion. She wrote an open letter to her sisters in Islam. Here is an edited version:

Polygamy is devastating for the women and children impacted. The bottom line is that polygamy is illegal in Canada. It is not a tenet of our faith. Equality means full rights as a citizen in the matters of the state, as well as equality within the family. The practice of polygamy is inherently harmful to women and children. It must be stopped. Women are being told to accept it as their religious duty and that it is mandated by our faith. This is not true!

My advice: Be yourself. You are in charge of who you are. You are not what happened to you. You are not a product. You are not a commodity. You are not your father's honour. You are a blessing from Allah. You are not your husband's honour. You are your husband's equal companion and confidante. You are not your brother's honour. You are equal

to your brother. You have an equal right to
education and your family's resources. You
are not your son's "honour." You are your
son's life source. Reclaim your identity. Don't
let others dictate your purpose. Don't let others decide your worth or your contributions.
Spiritual equality is your God-given right.

There's a flip side to this heartfelt plea to protect women from bad marriages. It comes from
Cosmopolitan, the cheeky magazine whose former
editor Helen Gurley Brown brought us *Sex and
the Single Girl*, which scandalized America when
it was published in 1962. The magazine is now
headlining the "Instagram relationship." Marriage
might have been a practical solution based on
deal-making between families, likely during the
agriculture era, when formalized relationships
began, but it morphed into romantic love during
the late seventeenth and early eighteenth centuries. However, two-thirds of university women
surveyed in 1967 said they'd marry someone they
didn't love if he met other criteria, such as financial
security. Then, between 1990 and 2015, the divorce
rate doubled among those fifty and up, propelled
by the baby boomers. The trending news is that

twenty-first-century marriages are better called transactional relationships. Looking for security (a.k.a. a rich guy)? Or for parenthood (because the clock is ticking)? Or a quick divorce (because it's inevitable)? Here are the tools of the TR, says *Cosmo*: rocketlawyer.com, where couples can create customized prenuptial agreements; seeking.com, which advertises with the tagline "Relationships on your terms" and states that its customers "are up front about their expectations"; and wevorce.com, offering a "peaceful, collaborative divorce" in thirty days for a reasonable price, no lawyers needed.

Also up front are women taking their newfound power to control their own bodies to an extent we could hardly have imagined years ago. Janice Boddy, a professor of anthropology at the University of Toronto, wrote a stunning research paper in 2016 that compares the ills of female genital cutting to new surgical interventions called labiaplasty and vaginal rejuvenation. Labiaplasty involves surgically trimming the labia minora (inner lips) and sometimes the labia majora (outer lips) of the vulva. It is typically performed on women under the age of thirty-five to make their bodies look more tucked in instead of messy or protruding. Vaginal rejuvenation is performed on older women who have given birth in the past and feel their vaginas are too loose or too wide — typically to tighten them up for sexual reasons, to give more pleasure to their partners. It means altering labia minora that have elongated with age, tightening a vagina that's become slack with childbirth, plumping up the outer labia with lipo-injection, and de-roofing a clitoris that's started drooping.

"What worries me most is that a percentage of these operations are being performed on girls under the age of 18 with parental consent, which is similar to the situation I was looking at when I was studying female genital cutting in Sudan," says Boddy. "Women in Europe, the Americas, New Zealand, and Australia — places that led the campaign against FGM — are discovering their genitals to be 'abnormal': disproportioned, messy, lacking symmetry," she reports in HAU: *Journal of Ethnographic Theory*. She calls this "a widespread cultural denial of aging, or even becoming adult . . . in that the desired outcome is for genitals resembling those of a prepubescent girl."

Activists have been shadowboxing with political, cultural, and religious forces for decades to sort out the consequences of controlling your own body and exercising the right to decide what's good for you. While labiaplasty isn't up there with life-and-death procedures, it does illustrate how the disruptors have in many ways created a new space.

Imagine what Aristotle or Thomas Aquinas would have to say about this. It has been suggested that women want to toss the old traditions and customs into the ditch, along with religions that have served them badly. That is not true. Women, in fact, are usually the keepers of the keys when it comes to customs, and there are not more devout men than there are women when it comes to religion. I recently read a tweet written by an Afghan man about an article I had penned for the *Globe and Mail* about the detrimental effect on women and girls of the Taliban-U.S. peace talks being held in the absence of the Afghan government. He said I was a hypocrite who had no regard for the religion or the country, and that all I cared about was the women. His accusation reminded me of the famous quote from Sarah Grimké, an abolitionist and feminist from South Carolina. Her father was an attorney and a judge, and she wanted to pursue the same career — but he forbade her. In an 1837 letter, she wrote: "I ask no favors for my sex. I surrender not our claim to equality. All I ask of our brethren is, that they will take their feet from off our necks and permit us to stand upright on that ground which God designed us to occupy." One hundred and eighty-two years later, the iconic U.S. Supreme Court Justice Ruth Bader Ginsberg repeated those words in the opening of the documentary RBG, which hails her as a cultural icon and a hero for justice and women: "All I ask of our brethren is, that they will take their feet from off our necks."

CHAPTER FOUR

WHEN THE PATRIARCHY
MEETS THE MATRIARCHY

IN 2003, CAROLYN BENNETT, then chairwoman of
the women's caucus in Jean Chrétien's Liberal government, was commenting to the media that the
prime minister had appointed a Chinese-Canadian
woman to be governor general (Adrienne Clarkson)
and a woman as chief justice on the Supreme Court
(Beverley McLachlin). She also said, "However, he
has nine male cabinet ministers, and that's not a
very good optic for women." The press dropped the
first part of her remark, quoting only the last part.
In a private caucus meeting soon after, Chrétien
took her apart verbally. In fact, the dressing-down
was so severe that other members of the caucus
leaked it to the press.

I had been working on a profile of Bennett, a physician turned member of parliament, and had been following her around her riding, watching her at community events. She was invariably stopped by schoolkids ranging from age six to sixteen who said, "Hi, Dr. Bennett, you delivered me." Later, I scheduled a lengthy interview with her. I asked her how frightened she had been when the prime minister yelled at her in front of her colleagues. She thought for a few seconds and then said, "I'll tell you what fear is: fear is when the baby's elbow is stuck in the birth canal; fear is when the fetal heart rate drops. This other business — that's politics."

The motto of Women's College Hospital in Toronto, where Bennett worked, is *Non quo sed quomodo* — Not what we do, but how. She remembers a time when hospital policies were made for the convenience of the doctor. But, she says, "At Women's College, the policies were determined by listening to everyone — to nurses and committee members and patients." She remembers a patient who had an appendicitis attack just after having delivered a baby and going back home. She went back to the hospital and had surgery. In those days, she should have been placed in the surgical ward, which would have meant leaving the baby behind.

"But we prided ourselves in busting old rules," said Bennett. "The newborn couldn't be with her on the surgical floor. Clearly she had to go to the maternity floor. Any other decision would be for the convenience of the doctor."

Bennett believes both politics and policies change when people listen to all concerned. As the current minister of Crown–Indigenous Relations and Northern Affairs, she sees this practised in Indigenous communities. They pass the talking stick — they get everyone's ideas before making a decision. "In politics," she says, "when you add women, you change policies. The *what* changes — so does the *how*. Men are afraid to talk about breast cancer, child abuse, violence — add women [to the conversation] and those [issues] will get discussed."

"Democracy is messy," she says. "Women understand messy."

TOWARD THE END of a tumultuous 2018, the secretary-general of the United Nations, António Guterres, said, "Our world is suffering from a bad case of trust deficit disorder." He pointed out that we've lost trust in leaders, national institutions, and rules based on global order. He even claimed that trust is at a breaking point: "Today, world order is increasingly chaotic. Power relations are less clear. Universal values are being eroded."

He was, of course, referring diplomatically to the worrisome appeal of populists. Populism supposedly speaks to the "people" and against the "elite." Populists lean on the fears and anxieties and insecurities of people who vote for them. They want more cops, more prisons, fewer taxes. They say, "Here's who to blame for your troubles; now vote for me." Although the term has been around since the nineteenth century and has been presented from both the political left and the right, in twenty-first-century politics it was hijacked by supposed champions of the little guy, portraying themselves as wizards with all the answers and as purveyors of blame.

Jamie Bartlett, senior fellow at Demos, a public policy think tank in the U.K., says that "populism has two chief characteristics. First, it offers immediate and supposedly obvious answers to complicated problems, which usually blame some other group along the way. Second, it claims to represent the decent but downtrodden 'people' against a corrupt and distant elite . . . Social media provide the perfect platform for both lines of attack."

But Bartlett also reminds us that there was a time when "Nicholas Negroponte — former director of the illustrious MIT Media Lab — declared in 1997 that the internet would bring about world peace, and the end of nationalism."

As far back as 1892, the U.S. had a political movement called the Populist Party that contributed to constitutional amendments such as a progressive tax system. In the twentieth century, Juan Perón of Argentina and Hugo Chávez of Venezuela led populist movements that appealed to ordinary people who felt their concerns were ignored by the elites. Fascism also had populist appeal. It became clear with the election of populists after 2010 that as a governing style it is invariably detrimental to those who seek equality rights — women the world over. Carolyn Bennett, now a twenty-two-year veteran politician, says, "Populism is dangerous for women. It foments toxic masculinity and the angry white man. While there are women who participate in it, it has an ugly racist, misogynist, homophobic core."

Spokespeople for the unspeakable gained access to huge audiences. Racism, xenophobia, misogyny, fear-mongering, and outright lies became the new trend in public rhetoric. When Donald Trump was elected president of the United States in November 2016, it triggered a firestorm among women everywhere and created the biggest call to arms the world's women have ever seen. The turmoil around him — affairs with adult film stars and models, boasting about grabbing women by the pussy, poking fun at the disabled, mean-mouthing women who menstruate — created a political power shift for women.

Women have been trying to move the dial to equality rights for thousands of years — they left handprints on the cave walls during the Stone Age by way of saying, "I was here." They raised their voices for women and girls in the industrial age to remind the innovators not to leave half the population behind, and they led waves of change as suffragettes and baby boomers. These were pieces of the kindling that social scientists say is required for major sustainable change. The eruption begins when the bundles of kindling come together and turn into an accumulation of all that has gone before. The election of Donald Trump was the match that lit the bonfire during the fourth wave of the women's movement. Social media amplified the voices and fanned the flames.

Women began using personal power — the kind that says, "What *you* are doing is not okay with *me*" — to speak up in the public square, at the workplace, and in the kitchen, with no-nonsense demands, well-researched theories, and politically powerful backing like never before. The Women's March on Washington in 2017 was a direct reaction to the election of Donald Trump, and it attracted five million women who marched in cities around the world. And women in record numbers signed up to run for political office and won. They began to fight back against bullies and sexual harassers and men who see women as objects, as extras, as superfluous.

Historically, populists pick on outsiders such as immigrants and appeal to the anti-elites by evoking the good old days when coal heated our houses and gasoline was cheap and June Cleaver was in the kitchen in her apron, baking cherry pie. But an analysis of populist party lines shows they also take direct aim at women's equality rights to stir up their supporters — those who are anti-choice or oppose working mothers, for example. Although the populists interpreted their victory as a win for the politics of disruption, women saw that same disruption as an opportunity to rewrite the playbook, to recreate their roles in public debate, and to redefine policies.

Populism reminds one of the words of the late Isaac Asimov, the American scientist and writer, who said of the U.S., "The strain of anti-intellectualism has been a constant thread winding its way through our political and cultural life, nurtured by the false notion that democracy means that 'my ignorance is just as good as your knowledge.'"

Kenneth Roth, the executive director of Human Rights Watch, said, "In this cauldron of discontent, certain politicians are flourishing and even gaining power by portraying rights as protecting only the terrorist suspect or the asylum seeker at the expense of the safety, economic welfare, and cultural preferences of the presumed majority. They scapegoat refugees, immigrant communities, and minorities. Truth is a frequent casualty. Nativism, xenophobia, racism, and Islamophobia are on the rise." And he warns, "This dangerous trend threatens to reverse the accomplishments of the modern human rights movement."

It certainly threatens women who are being confronted with verbal assaults and draconian policies that seem to be burping out of an old boys' network gone rogue. The president of the United States says it's okay to "grab her by the pussy." He's joined by luminaries such as Brazil's President

Jair Bolsonaro, also known as the "Trump of the Tropics," who once told a congresswoman, "I'm not going to rape you, because you're very ugly," and the president of the Philippines, Rodrigo Duterte, who told soldiers that they could each rape up to three women with impunity and they should shoot female rebels "in the vagina."

The leaders of Poland, Hungary, and Italy are following the populist suit. Research from American political commentator Peter Beinart claims the new authoritarians are waging war on women; he says that "no matter how high a woman ascends, she's ultimately just a body whose value is determined by men."

Valerie Hudson, a political scientist at Texas A&M University, says the simple issue governing all these acts is that "men agreed to be ruled by other men in return for all men ruling over women." That comment takes us back to the birth of patriarchy ten thousand years ago, when men began to acquire women because they needed labourers and only women could reproduce. The empowerment of women, particularly over the past decades, has overruled that appropriation and challenged the domination of men.

That's what's stirring the authoritarian men when

they win the leadership stakes — they quickly turn on women. They use typical attacks — humiliating powerful women, blaming women, encouraging women to remain subservient to men.

For example, with Poland's impressively high numbers of professional women and one of the lowest pay gaps in the European Union, one would expect the country to leap away from its authoritarian past, and for a while it did. I was in Warsaw in 2015 for the launch of the Polish edition of my book *Ascent of Women* (published there under the title *Wojna kobiet*, which means "War of Women") and felt the rising tide of feminism and the shedding of the oppressive power of the Catholic Church. There was an all-things-can-happen air when I talked to women in the media about the opportunities ahead. But there was also an unspoken fear that the women's movement could be hijacked. The jubilant conversations were taking place without the cheer of victory; there was a check-over-your-shoulder aspect to the emancipation. And sure enough, when the Law and Justice party (Prawo i Sprawiedliwość, or PiS) became the majority in the parliament in 2015, within months of my visit, the fears of Polish women were realized. The Ministry of Health launched an ad campaign telling women to "breed like rabbits." The government has launched measures attacking reproductive rights, including a ban on emergency contraception and another bill to ban abortion, and it has assailed LGBTQ rights and organizations. Now the PiS party is attacking women's rights activists and organizations through raids on their offices, denial of funding, public smear campaigns, and disciplinary action. And as most populists do, they're selling their anti-women concept under the banner of family values, which is short form for "stay at home, produce children, and stop seeking change."

In Italy, when Prime Minister Giuseppe Conte was elected in 2018, he appointed an interior minister who is anti-immigration and a health and disability minister who opposes abortion and same-sex marriage. Then the city council of Verona voted in favour of financing anti-abortion programs.

Hungary's prime minister, Viktor Orbán, made headlines by vowing to eliminate taxes for any woman who has four or more children. He brushed aside wide-scale protests led by women, stating that "we want Hungarian children. Migration for us is surrender." This is a leader who demands that women conform to traditional gender roles. In 2015, when asked why there were no women in his cabinet, he asserted that few women can deal with the stress of politics. Two years later, after withdrawing his female U.S. ambassador, Réka Szemerkényi, he avoided questions by saying he would not comment on "women's issues." And in 2018 he effectively banned the teaching of gender studies across the country.

WOMEN ARE FIGHTING BACK. In Italy they are pointing an accusatory finger at the Catholic Church and carrying placards that read, "Keep your rosaries off my ovaries."

But the biggest response to populism has been #MeToo and #TimesUp. When actor Alyssa Milano picked up Tarana Burke's phrase "Me Too" and turned it into a hashtag, she was soon joined by other Hollywood stars, including Jennifer Lawrence, Ashley Judd, and Gwyneth Paltrow. That was October 2017. In November 2017, the Alianza Nacional de Campesinas wrote a letter from 700,000 female farmworkers in the U.S. and sent it as a sign of solidarity to the Hollywood women involved in exposing sexual abuse. On November 10, 2017, *Time* published the letter, launching #TimesUp, a movement supporting people — women, men, people of colour, members of the LGBTQ community — who want to speak up about harassment but lack funding and media access.

Both hashtags went viral. Within weeks, French women were tweeting #BalanceTonPorc (rat out your pig), and in Italy it became #QuellaVoltaChe (that time when . . .). Even China had #WoYeShi (me too). The movement quickly moved from Hollywood, where powerful men like Harvey Weinstein had coerced aspiring young actors into sex, to the music industry, sports, and Wall Street and Bay Street, where some men were so shaken by the movement they started worrying about having lunch with female colleagues, lest they be accused of improper behaviour. That echoed the longstanding habit of Vice President Mike Pence, who made headlines after becoming vice-president by stating he would never have a meeting alone with a woman. Why not? Can it be that he is so unable to control his lust that he dares not break bread with a female? Or does he think she'll make his head spin and fool him into changing his mind about a policy?

The reaction against populism picked up speed in Slovakia in March 2019, when Zuzana Čaputová was elected president and delivered her acceptance speech in Slovak as well as Hungarian, Czech, Roma, and Ruthenian (an East Slavic dialect) — languages of the nation's minority groups. In doing so, she set herself apart by putting the boot to the nationalist rants in neighbouring countries. She had already made her name as a fighter for justice because of a fourteen-year legal battle she waged as a lawyer against a company that had plans to build an illegal landfill site in her hometown. She won the case, and the nickname "Slovakia's Erin Brockovich," after the environmental campaigner played by Julia Roberts in the film of the same name. In the run-up to the presidential election, she ignored issues such as immigration and family values, which the populist parties had been campaigning on, and called for greater LGBTQ rights.

A weapon that women hold is their seemingly innate ability to "girlfriend" — to band together and identify an issue and then make and execute a plan with lightning speed. For example, when Mike Pence was named VP in 2016, everyone knew he was looking for a way to force Planned Parenthood out of business. The fact that they supply free mammograms and health care to poor women didn't matter to Pence. He was after the organization because some of its funding goes toward abortion services. Ruthless in his pursuit of shutting down Planned Parenthood — he'd been gunning for them long before he rode into Washington — now he had the power of the White House behind him. But he also had a powerful opponent — the women who said, "Not on my watch." It was one of those morning-after stories that left everyone shaking their heads at the same time, asking where to sign on. On November 9, 2016, American women began to send donations to Planned Parenthood in the name of Mike Pence. They sent $5 and $20 and $500. Actor Mila Kunis pledged a donation every month in the name of Mike Pence. Which meant Pence would receive a thank-you note for every single donation, large or small. By December, Planned Parenthood had received 315,000 donations, and more than 82,000 were made in Mike Pence's name. At the same time, grey mailbags stuffed with thank-you notes were being delivered to the Office of the Vice President of the United States at the White House, 1600 Pennsylvania Avenue, Washington, DC.

At the time of writing, the American Civil Liberties Union and Planned Parenthood have filed a lawsuit against the government of Alabama over the abortion ban law that is supposed to take effect in November 2019. They claim the law violates the right to liberty and privacy under the Fourteenth Amendment to the U.S. Constitution.

SOME WONDERED IF the #MeToo movement could keep up the momentum, but two years later, women and girls around the world have vowed to continue to march, to tweet, to keep this kettle boiling until the sexual offenders are exposed and held accountable for assault and bullying and putting women down. As much as men like Weinstein carried out their disgusting acts quietly and with impunity, it was the internet that amplified women's voices. They took a page out of the disruptors' playbook and busted up some old presumptions about women who work for bosses who grope and CEOs who pay them less than a man for doing the same job, and women who play for coaches who see them as objects for sale. While there are a lot of disruptors on the scene — the environmentalists, the LGBTQ community, the left, not to mention religious extremists and political rabble-rousers like Marine La Pen — disruption has also created an opening for women to strike down old styles and old standards and old beliefs and old dependencies. When the door to disruption was opened by men like Trump, women from Moscow to Montreal saw it as an invitation to tweet, talk, and speed-dial their way into a fairer, safer, more just tomorrow.

The thing about standing up on a stage and speaking for all the world to hear is that it brings truth to the adage that if you can't talk about it, you can't change it. As much as women around the world are talking now about a major shift in our cultural attitudes and to the status quo, I'm often asked after a speech or a panel discussion, "What about the men? How do men feel about the level of emancipation spreading around the world?"

Immense changes are happening in the lives of men. Whereas men in the West are more accustomed to an altering status quo, men in places like Egypt, Lebanon, Morocco, and Palestine either see it as a burden or ignore it. "Understanding Masculinities" is the first study of its kind that takes a direct aim at men and women between the ages of eighteen and fifty-nine in the region known as MENA (Middle East and North Africa). In 2017, it addressed the shifting status and the crossroads men and women find themselves at today. These are not places that are rocking gently with the passage of time; conflict, poverty, and natural disasters such as prolonged droughts are menacing the region. So are high unemployment, political uncertainty, and economic instability. As the report says, "Men, in particular, are highly conflicted, holding to a past that no longer fits the present, and frequently uncertain about or unwilling to accept change that might ease their heavy burden of societally imposed patriarchal duty."

The report begins with a heartfelt message from Mohammad Naciri, regional director of Arab states for the United Nations Entity for Gender Equality and the Empowerment of Women: "I am humbled and inspired daily by the brave women and girls who defy the restrictive norms and expectations under which they live to speak up, stand up, and push forward for their rights — because that is what they do." He's referring to the staggering statistics — of women's low participation rates in economic and political life, of pervasive violence in private and public spheres alike, of tremendous societal pressure to conform to a very narrow definition of femininity and of women and girls persisting, counting small victories along the way. But, he says, "We have seen progress. Governments in the region have pushed for equality; particularly in the last few years, they have adopted legislation to ensure equal rights, they have criminalized violence against women, and some have lifted all reservations on CEDAW [the UN Convention on the Elimination of All Forms of Violence Against Women]. Still, the biggest obstacle of all is society: you and me and our neighbours, and the stereotypes and norms we harbour and perpetuate. We are all guilty of it, which is what makes those defiant women and girls all the more brave."

The facts are bewildering. Men are the pillars of patriarchies cross the MENA region. They "make most of the major household decisions . . . expect to control their wives' personal freedoms, from what they wear, to where they go, to when the couple has sex." In the street, "Violence and sexual harassment . . . are common for women across the region . . . The roots of gender-based violence . . . are found in women's limited power, in violence-supportive attitudes, and in highly violent childhoods."

Although a majority of men support "a wide array of inequitable, traditional attitudes . . . a sizeable minority — a quarter or more of men in each of the countries surveyed — show support for at least some dimensions of women's equality and empowerment." The majority of women, meanwhile, "not only affirm but also appear to accept male guardianship."

The report concluded that despite these discouraging facts, gender equality is possible; it is not a "foreign import," as so many have insisted, "but rather can emerge from the societies themselves, given the right circumstances."

I have worked with women in this region, written their stories, fundraised for their brand-new feminist centres, worried when they were arrested for bogus crimes like speaking about rights for women, watched with admiration as they tried to change the future for their daughters. I have also talked to the men, who feel pressure from the community to treat their wives and daughters the same way their fathers treated their mothers and sisters. As much as I shake my head in dismay at the view these men have of the women and want to (and sometimes do) speak my mind to them, I do not believe it is blind adherence to violence and oppression. I believe it is fear of change. And the women in MENA are talking the talk and walking the walk; they are moving steadfastly toward change, and every year a few more men walk with them.

ONE YEAR AFTER DONALD TRUMP moved into the White House, his erstwhile prophet, the redoubtable Steve Bannon, was quoted in the 2018 paperback edition of journalist Joshua Green's book *Devil's Bargain*, "Women are gonna take charge of society. And they couldn't juxtapose a better villain than Trump. He *is* the patriarch." What's more, reported *Business Insider*, Bannon "is reportedly terrified of the #MeToo movement — and thinks Oprah Winfrey poses an existential threat to President Donald Trump." His prediction, as paraphrased by Green: "The 2020 election wouldn't be merely the Democrats versus the Republicans, but the Patriarchy versus the Matriarchy."

On September 5, 1995, his future nemesis, Hillary Clinton, stood up in front of a worldwide audience at the Fourth World Conference on Women in Beijing and made the claim that women's rights are human rights. She'd been pressured to soften her remarks to avoid upsetting the Chinese. Instead, in front of delegates from 180 countries, she said, "If there is one message that echoes forth from this conference, let it be that human rights are women's rights and women's rights are human rights, once and for all." The words were a variation on a passage first written in the 1830s by abolitionist and proto-feminist Sarah Grimké, then used again in the 1980s by Marcella Maxwell when she was head of the New York City Human Rights Commission, by the Chilean jurist Cecilia Medira in 1985, and by Canada's Ed Broadbent while he was head of the International Centre for Human Rights and Democratic Development in 1993.

"As long as discrimination and inequities remain so commonplace everywhere in the world, as long as girls and women are valued less, fed less, fed last, overworked, underpaid, not schooled, subjected to violence in and outside their homes — the potential of the human family to create a peaceful, prosperous world will not be realized," Clinton said. The women delegates at the conference pounded on the tables and cheered.

There have been enormous changes to the political scene since women started aiming at a "critical mass." A long-held theory says that 30 percent representation is the magic number for changing the culture in a group. "More women in politics leads to more inclusive decisions and can change people's image of what a leader looks like," says UN Women's executive director Phumzile Mlambo-Ngcuka. "We still have a steep road ahead, but the growing proportion of women ministers is encouraging, especially where we see a rise in the number of countries with gender-balanced ministerial cabinets. These are the types of bold moves that we need if we are to dramatically increase women's representation in decision-making."

Women have worked for decades to get parliaments and legislative bodies to that 30 percent level. While critical mass theory doesn't have scientific proof, it's easy to imagine that if women made up 30 percent of the elected officials, the political behaviour would change, becoming less adversarial and more woman-friendly and gender-considerate.

It was Harvard business professor Rosabeth Kanter who first suggested in 1977 that there would be culture change in politics if 30 percent of the politicians were women. Whether more women meant a kinder, gentler setting or women sticking together and voting as a bloc, or both, that's not what happened. However, critical mass theory has fuelled the push for gender quotas around the world, based on the argument that more women are needed in politics before individual legislators can have an impact in gendered policy debates.

University of Toronto political science professor Sylvia Bashevkin disputes this. "Having 30 percent or more women in a given institution (critical mass) often matters less for getting equality interests represented than relying on the feminist consciousness and commitment of a lone individual (the critical actor)," she says. "We have only to consider the massive contributions of Judy LaMarsh in the 1960s as the sole woman in a federal cabinet (and among the very few female MPs in parliament at the time) that created the Royal Commission on the Status of Women, introduced national social policies such as healthcare, and created a national pension system. In short, numbers can be very misleading."

In most countries, the 30 percent threshold has not been met. According to some researchers, what they call "fast-track countries" — those that have experienced recent conflict or are moving toward democracy — have outpaced old democracies by legislating a percentage of women representatives. For example, as of February 2019, women made up 53.1 percent of the legislature in Bolivia, and in Rwanda it was 61.3 percent, whereas Canada's number was 26.9 percent and the U.K.'s was 32 percent. As the political representation of women increases, the culture in parliaments and legislatures does begin to change.

While the 30 percent factor still eludes women

in most countries, the global number of women elected as politicians has increased, and other measures tell a more encouraging story. According to the Inter-Parliamentary Union (IPU) and UN Women, as of January 1, 2019, women represent a higher percentage of government ministers worldwide than ever before, at 20.7 percent, and they are covering an increasingly diverse range of portfolios — compared to 2017, 30 percent more women handle defence portfolios, 52.9 percent more run finance, and 13.6 percent more run foreign affairs. The number of women parliamentary speakers is slightly up, as is the number of deputy speakers. Representation in top-level leadership is down, however: in 2017, 7.2 percent of elected heads of state were women, but that number's down to 6.6 percent; the proportion of women heads of government has dropped from 5.7 to 5.2 percent.

Gabriela Cuevas Barron, a Mexican MP and president of the IPU, said, "Equal representation in government positions is fundamental for a democracy to be truly representative and effective. Despite some positive movement, the overwhelming majority of government leaders remain male."

Proponents of critical mass say it's well accepted and is working as a tool for change. But some scholars suggest concentrating on two links that can really make a difference. First, they propose shifting the central research question from "when women make a difference" to "how the substantive representation of women occurs." Second, they condone moving the analytical focus from the macro to the micro level, replacing attempts to discern "what women do" with study of "what specific actors do."

And that's where the difference lies in the way women practise politics. Carolyn Bennett says we need to reframe the questions we ask: "As women we don't say: 'What's the matter with him?' We say instead, 'What happened to him?' As mothers we know that tough love doesn't work. We also know that restorative justice does work. We need to see the issues from all sides."

A government that considers all citizens comes to different conclusions, which leads to different policies. For example, I remember when the discussions around parental leave began in Canada. Some proposed lowering the school age from six years to three and establishing a maternity leave that would allow a mother to be with the child until age three. Canada has been moving in the right direction — most provinces have lowered the school age to four years — and the 2017 federal budget introduced an eighteen-month maternity leave. But it's traditionally been women who have to take the time off, which disrupts their career paths. The federal government launched a program in 2019 that allows a second parent to collect five additional weeks of employment insurance benefit, or eight weeks at a reduced rate. Prior to the change, both parents were free to share the months of leave as they saw fit.

According to Ivona Hideg, associate professor of organizational behaviour and human resource management at Wilfrid Laurier University, "The vast majority of the time was claimed by mothers. This new plan allocates these extra weeks exclusively to fathers or second parents . . . Based on experience in Quebec and other countries that already operate similar programs, when the second parent (which in most households is the father) is offered parental benefits on a use-it-or-lose-it basis, he or she overwhelmingly chooses to use it. More than 80 percent of Quebec's new dads take at least some portion of their parental benefit, compared to 12 percent of fathers in the rest of Canada." But the other benefit comes from considering the working mom's career. Hideg says working moms have "long faced an unfair career penalty simply because they shoulder the bulk of child-rearing duties. Plenty of research demonstrates that the longer a woman is away from paid work, the less likely she is to advance through promotions or pay increases once she returns." When men take more paternity leave, women are likelier to maintain full-time employment, the wage gap shrinks, and senior leadership positions on boards are occupied by more women. The employer gains a competitive edge in a diverse marketplace, and the men no longer limit themselves to the role of financial provider.

Still more evidence shows that the presence of women in politics is changing the status quo. In fact, you could say there's been a surge in women's involvement in politics, and women are using personal will to push public and political will. For example, after the #MeToo movement took off in October 2017, the film and television awards ceremonies that followed that winter and spring saw actresses dressed all in black, showing solidarity with their sisters. Similarly, at the State of the Union Address in January 2018, the Democratic women's caucus wore black. Then, in February 2019, following the momentous mid-term elections, the Democrat women, who were now members of the majority party in the House of Representatives, turned up in white — the symbolic shade of women's suffrage. White women, brown women, Black women, Native American women, and Asian women stood together in homage to the women who got the vote in 1920, as well as the African-American women who were denied the vote until 1965. When President Donald Trump announced that 58 percent of the new jobs created in America had gone to women — boasting as though he had personally created the jobs — the women jumped to their feet, stood together laughing, and pointed at each other, because they were a part of that job gain. And he had indeed had a hand in their election to office. They did what women do best — they drew the attention away from him and gave it to all Americans, shouting, "USA! USA! USA!" — the very chant Trump had hijacked in his presidency, encouraging his huge Make-America-Great-Again crowd. It was quite a night — women, writ large, were unleashed on the most politically important night of the year.

The idea of having 30 percent women in legislative assemblies spread to the corporate world in 2010, when Dame Helena Morrissey started what she called the 30% Club in the U.K. According to the club's vision statement, "gender balance on corporate boards and senior management not only encourages better leadership and governance, but diversity further contributes to better all-round board performance, and ultimately increased corporate performance [a.k.a. profit] for both companies and their shareholders." The club has become a global initiative, with fourteen chapters around the world. The one in Canada was founded by Spencer Lanthier, former CEO of KPMG. At a seminar at the Rotman School of Management in Toronto, Lanthier recalls that an executive was asked why there were no women on his board. He replied that they had "done a global search and could not find a qualified woman." Lanthier says the man was virtually booed out of the room, so he decided to get the ball rolling and launched the Canadian chapter of the 30% Club in 2014. The U.S. club launched the same year with Peter Grauer, chair of Bloomberg LP, as the founder. The club reports that in 2019, "26.9% of S&P 100 directors are women, up from 20.2% at launch. Additionally, all S&P 100 boards have at least one female director. While the S&P 100 is on track to achieve the 30% target by 2020 the numbers are moving at a glacial pace."

As the 30% Club's website reports, "A critical

barrier for women seeking board appointments is a lack of connections and access to sitting board members who have influence over the nomination and selection of directors." Club members enlist support from public corporations and other significant players in the capital markets, such as major pension plans. There are no membership fees and no mandatory quotas, only an interest in "meaningful, sustainable gender balance in business."

"The progress has been much slower than I had hoped," says Lanthier. "For example, the oil patch has been very resistant to get on board and offers the same invalid reasons for not supporting women at the board level." He also warns, "If the current pace doesn't pick up, we will see regulatory intervention by governments and security commissions. The State of California is a recent constituency mandating minimum levels of gender diversity." The club members prefer using behind-the-scenes persuasion to help make boards more representative. He says they have already seen the difference diversity makes, and hopes over time the organization will be called the 50% Club. "Would you only hire from individuals born between January 1 and June 30? Why leave out half the population from your talent pool? It makes no sense." The philosophy of the club is that "what gets measured gets managed — a numeric goal provides real impetus for change," and they plan to reach it by 2022.

IN 2014, THE SWEDISH GOVERNMENT launched an approach to a feminist foreign policy it called "3R": rights, representation, and resources. "Rights" meant that women's issues, including violence and discrimination, would be publicized. "Representation" would involve support for women who occupied decision-making positions in both the private and public sectors. "Resources" indicated that funding would be allocated equitably.

Sweden has long been ahead of the pack when it comes to women's issues, even coining the term "feminist foreign policy." In a March 2015 *New Yorker* interview, Swedish Foreign Minister Margot Wallström said that a feminist foreign policy means "standing against the systematic and global subordination of women." The relationship between the inclusion of women in politics and success at the peace table has long been demonstrated by the United Nations, academic journals, and military publications. It is also known that

peace agreements signed without women's participation are likelier to fail. And we know from the
30% Club that having women in positions of economic leadership means a better bottom line for
the corporate world. McKinsey & Company, in a
2015 study, determined that a stunning $28 trillion
could be added to global GDP by 2025 if women par-
ticipated at the same rate as men.

Other countries quickly followed suit. As of
June 2019, eighty national governments had action
plans to increase women's roles in peace and security processes. Australia, Finland, the U.K., the
U.S., and other nations have envoy positions for
women's issues in a bid to promote gender equality internationally. Women's empowerment is
now an explicit part of the foreign aid programs of
Australia and France. The first-ever feminist international assistance policy was launched in 2018 in
Canada. According to Global Affairs Canada, "The
Feminist Foreign Policy recognizes that fostering
rights-based, open and inclusive societies, where all
people, regardless of their gender, can fully benefit from equal participation in economic, political,
social and cultural life, is an effective way to build
a safer and more prosperous world."

Governments are scrambling to respond to

the vast changes for women and to direct foreign policy accordingly. When Prime Minister Justin Trudeau announced his first cabinet, it was 50 percent women. When asked why, he said, "Because it's 2015." Announcing to the world that the federal cabinet would be 50 percent women "because it's 2015" was one step. But it was another giant leap to dedicate a $650 million fund to assisting women around the world, immediately after Donald Trump used his ill-gotten power to undermine women's health with the "global gag rule," which stripped health care to women and cut services for infant and child health. And then, at the Women Deliver international conference in Vancouver in June 2019, a stunning $300 million was announced as the new Equality Fund for women at home and abroad—the largest single government contribution made to women's rights in history. And the government bumped up international spending on women's health from $1.1 billion to $1.4 billion by 2023. Within that amount, the funds for women's sexual and reproductive health increase from $300 million to $700 million.

The unfortunate conclusion is that the president of the United States stands close to anti-woman groups like the Taliban in Afghanistan, ISIS in

Iraq, and Boko Haram in Nigeria on hateful policies toward women. Much of the rest of the world has installed foreign policy to address the fact that women are propelling changes immense enough to tackle such intractable problems as poverty, conflict, and violence — files that can turn the economy around. The number of girls attending school is higher than ever before; women are negotiating peace, which means treaties are more sustainable; and courses and think tanks are helping men become aware of the role they play in stopping violence against women.

The Canadian government's foreign policy has even waded into internecine battles by providing funds for organizations such as Canadian Women for Women in Afghanistan, which works toward getting Afghan girls to school, and to Journalists for Human Rights, which trains women journalists in places such as South Sudan to take on injustices and alter the status quo, along with the direction of the civil war.

When OpenCanada.org asked women around the world to comment on a feminist foreign policy, here's what some of them said:

JACINDA ARDERN, PRIME MINISTER of New Zealand: It means advocating strongly for women in international forums and working hard to meet our obligations in relation to the status of women. These include the United Nations Convention on the Elimination of All Forms of Discrimination against Women and the Beijing Declaration and Platform for Action, which sets goals for the global advancement of women . . . We are placed 9th out of 144 countries in the World Economic Forum's Global Gender Gap Index 2016. There are 46 women in the current parliament, 38.4 percent of the total 120 MPs, which is the highest representation in our history.

ELIN LISS, SWEDISH ACTIVIST and political scientist: A feminist foreign policy challenges power . . . it views conflict through a gendered lens and sees how patriarchal structures fuel violence and conflicts, especially in societies where masculinity is militarized. Therefore, a feminist foreign policy should be anti-militaristic and put human security at the centre . . . It chooses diplomacy over the use of force, preventing violent conflict instead of waging war . . . Feminist policy is about walking the walk and not just talking the talk.

OSAI OJIGHO, HUMAN RIGHTS LAWYER and director of Amnesty International Nigeria:
Feminist leadership is the responsible and accountable use of power to empower others . . . Power
as we know it, whether political or positional, is
vested in traditional institutions such as government and corporations. To restore equilibrium
in society and create meaningful participatory
engagement in the evolving global world, a feminist foreign policy draws attention to people, not
structures . . . When it concerns status and gender
relations between men and women, patriarchal values elevate the status of men to the detriment of
women. A feminist foreign policy must therefore
direct attention to areas that enhance the active
participation of all people, especially women.

MARIE-CLAUDE BIBEAU, CANADA'S former minister
of international development:
Local women's organizations that advance women's
rights . . . play an important role . . . That is why
[the government of Canada] launched the Women's
Voice and Leadership initiative as part of our new
Feminist International Assistance Policy, to support the crucial work of these local women's groups
in the Global South . . . the launch of this policy is

not the end of the process but rather a first step in a longer journey to achieving the best international assistance results.

MELANNE VERVEER, EXECUTIVE DIRECTOR, Georgetown University's Institute for Women, Peace and Security:
No country can get ahead if it leaves half its people behind . . . Advancing equal rights is a moral imperative — but it's strategic too. There is a wealth of research and data to show that investing in women is critical for economic, social and political progress. A foreign policy that puts women at its core — whether explicitly called feminist or not — helps tackle the most pressing global challenges.

J. ANN TICKNER, U.S.-BASED political scientist: The inclusion of women is at once strategic and just . . . An important dimension of any feminist foreign policy should be decreasing arms sales, particularly sales of the types of weapons that kill civilians, the majority of whom are women and children . . . The inclusion of women in diplomacy and peace building relies on two types of arguments: a rights-based approach, which claims that women deserve to be included, and an instrumental approach, which argues women bring something valuable to peace building, and that development goals more generally are more likely to be met if women's development is prioritized.

JAYNE STOYLES, EXECUTIVE DIRECTOR, Amnesty International Canada (English branch):
A feminist policy can guide all policymaking . . . A feminist foreign policy is the lawful thing to do to uphold international human rights standards. It is the smart thing to do to promote global peace and security, given that research shows peace processes are more lasting when women are involved. It is the prudent financial thing to do to address root causes, rather than perpetual Band-Aid solutions.

ANDREA GROBOCOPATEL, CO-CHAIR of the 2018 W20 in Argentina:
Choosing the evolution of society requires all of us as the driving force for change. In order to face a volatile and complex world, with rapid changes, marginalization, greed and environmental damage, both innovation and creativity are needed. This will be possible only if there are different points of

view and more diversity in decision-making, which is why we need to incorporate women's voices.

WHILE WE HAVE MOVED FORWARD, we are still surrounded by evidence of where we have failed. The past teaches us valuable lessons about the path to take in the future, but altering the laws and constitutional rights of those harmed by entrenched legislation is like untying a Gordian knot. An example would be the infamous Indian Act in Canada, under which all manner of human rights violations have been inflicted on generations of First Nations peoples, making them wards of the state and stripping them of land rights. Introduced in 1876, the act is steeped in the patriarchal beliefs and social expectations of the politicians who wrote it. They didn't take into consideration Indigenous women, who made up half the Indigenous population; compounding the insult was the fact that this was a mostly matrilineal society, with wealth and power passed down through the mother. For thousands of years before contact, women had not only been equal but had been wise Elders.

Mary Eberts, the trailblazing lawyer who has served as litigation counsel to the Native Women's

Association of Canada for more than twenty-five years, refers to the Act as "Victoria's Secret" because it was

> an enforcement of the Victorian family ideal at two levels depending on whether the woman married an Indian or non-Indian man. Indians in reserves were intended to have conventional Victorian unions, with the husband the controlling partner and the wife under his dominance. But the marriage of an Indian woman to a non-Indian man had great consequences; the Victorian "woman follows man" model was imposed with a vengeance. She was made to follow her mate right out of Indian status, the reserve, her band, and her family. And their children would not ever have status. This was a horrendous deprivation. Stripped of membership in her own band and required to leave with her husband, she was isolated from her own family and support system, and without legal recourse, she was vulnerable in cases of marital discord or family breakdown.

Mary Two-Axe Earley was a Mohawk woman from the reserve of Kahnawake, on the south shore of the St. Lawrence River. But when she married her non-status husband in 1929, she lost her rights and status under the Indian Act. In 1966 she became a leader of the Indigenous women's rights movement and fought a battle that lasted for nearly two decades. In June 1985, Bill C-31 was given royal assent, amending the Indian Act and reinstating some of the women who had lost their status through section 12(1)(b), which was known to Mary Two-Axe and her sisters as "the marrying-out clause." On July 5, 1985, when Two-Axe Earley's status was reinstated, she said, "Now I'll have legal rights again. After all these years, I'll be legally entitled to live on the reserve, to own property, die and be buried with my own people." Mary Two-Axe Earley died in 1996, leaving a legacy of change, but her example left a challenge for women to do more.

Part of that legacy is found in the final report of the National Inquiry into Missing and Murdered Indigenous Women and Girls, filed with the government of Canada in June 2019. The report concludes that the violence perpetrated against First Nations, Inuit, and Métis is the result of colonialism and

discrimination and constitutes a race-based genocide of Indigenous peoples. In Canada, the number
of missing and murdered Indigenous women and
girls is staggering. While a 2014 Royal Canadian
Mounted Police report found that 1,181 cases had
been reported to the police since 1980, Indigenous
women's groups say the accurate number is more
like 4,000. Indigenous women in the U.S. cite
similar figures. Questions are finally being asked:
Where are they? Who hurt them? Why were they
not on a missing persons list? And what are governments going to do about the racism and misogyny
that led to the violence?

"The staggering amount of violence against
Indigenous women is a product of colonialism,"
Eberts says.

> The Indian Act of Canada is a powerful and
> still operating instrument of colonialism and
> patriarchy. The Act has made Indigenous
> women legal nullities, placed them outside
> the rule of law, and the protection and benefit
> of the law, and taken them from their fam-
> ilies. In so doing the Act has produced or
> heightened the risk of harm in the lives of
> Indigenous women. When non-Indigenous

commentators allude to the "high-risk life-styles" of Indigenous women, they usually mean to imply that the women engage in prostitution. But in fact the lives of all Indigenous women are high risk: though the Indian Act does not cover Métis or Inuit, it is a powerful social influence that affects all Indigenous women even if they are not subject to it, because it carries out-moded Victorian ideas about all Indigenous women forward through time and pro-tects those ideas from the forces of social change, which might otherwise have mod-ulated them. The violence that permeates the lives of Indigenous women in Canada today is largely the result of the Indian Act, which functions to make Indigenous women a population of prey.

While Eberts's words touch on a single part of the tapestry of catastrophe affecting Indigenous women in Canada, the U.S., Australia, New Zealand, and other parts of the colonized world, they fit with so many notions of women that have led to wrong conclusions throughout history. The voices of Indigenous women are weaving the

threads of the past together, sharing their own stories and their own designs for the way forward.

BRINGING ALL THE VOICES of all the changemakers
to the table is the success of the fourth wave of the
women's movement. Intersectionality has become
the key to righting the wrongs for women. That's
why a feminist government — its policies and
practices — is becoming increasingly important in
governing all people. Poor women find it harder
to get elected. Disabled women face more violence
than able-bodied women. LGBTQ women have
encountered obstacles to receiving disaster relief.
Indigenous women are easily dismissed when it
comes to violence and racism. Muslim women have
to justify their religious beliefs. The list goes on.
When governments take all of us into account,
policies change. And that comes from asking different questions. The barriers faced by a middle-class
woman are different from the barriers faced by a
trans woman. Intersectionality means looking at
your own privilege, not in terms of who's better or
worse off than you but in terms of the discrimination that applies to each person.

That's why the issue of personal will is so

relevant to the politics women need to decipher today. I have noticed this in one assignment after another, in every country I have been reporting from: the political will and public will we have always used to make change have been overtaken by personal will. I used Malala Yousafzai as an example in chapter 1. Here's another example — the case I described in chapter 3 of the 160 girls in Kenya between the ages of three and seventeen who sued their government for failing to protect them from being raped — that court case began with the personal will of one twelve-year-old girl. There was no political or public will when it started. There are laws on the Kenyan books that make defilement a crime. But the men have impunity. Hardly anyone is ever arrested for rape. Almost no one goes to jail. The case actually started at a village meeting, when community members were discussing the need to build a school. A twelve-year-old girl called Milly stood up at the meeting and said, "I want to go to school. But I can't go to school because I'm pregnant and I'm pregnant because that man sitting over there raped me." She pointed at the guilty man sitting with the others from the community.

Personal will also has a powerful effect on the way politics affects the status of girls. When Boko

Haram kidnapped more than two hundred girls from Chibok, Nigeria, we saw something happen that had never happened before. U.S. President Barack Obama said he was sending strategic advisors and surveillance equipment to find the girls — he made history. No government, no military had ever sent anyone anywhere to rescue girls — ever. The message was clear: girls count, and education is paramount. Those girls are still in the news today. This is unheard of: we've gone from "who cares" to a worldwide demand to find those girls. It's true that the story could still have a tragic ending, but for those of us who follow the state of the world's girls, this was a step to remember.

There's more. I did a story for the *Ottawa Citizen* when that kidnapping happened. You'll recall that some of the girls escaped the day they were kidnapped. One of them was fourteen years old. She escaped by jumping off the back of the truck the girls had been put in. She rolled into the bush and tried to bury herself in debris. The Boko Haram thugs saw her jump and stopped the truck to search for her, poking long poles into the ground to see where she was hiding. Thankfully they didn't find her. My question to her was, how did you have the nerve to jump off a fast-moving truck? She answered immediately: "I figured I could only die once. If I stayed on the truck, they'd kill me. So I jumped."

I talked about this extraordinarily brave action with the others in the village (in a telephone conversation with an interpreter) and here's what they said: "These girls were in school. Some of them were graduating. They all had plans to go to university, to make something of themselves, and to come back to the village and solve the many problems we have." This is also personal will. And this is the kind of leadership that's making a powerful change in the world today.

Young women are talking in ways they haven't before. For example, the taboo against speaking out about sexual assault has been broken. Everyone knows that if you can't talk about it, you can't change it. Now they are talking.

This is the girl talk that's altering the relationship between political will, public will, and personal will. Political will may lag behind. Public will may surge ahead or retreat. But what salvages both of them is the person who stands up and says, "This is what I want." That electrifies the public and the political.

When you look at this as binary—the political and the public—it needs to be pushed by the personal: the individual who says, "What you're doing is not okay with me." This is what's driving the bus for women's and girls' rights. Equality law and gender advocacy and change depend on these individuals. The internet gives easy access to their stories. Social media inspire the public because people on Facebook, Twitter, and Instagram put up personal accounts that are the heart and soul of the story. This provides momentum and a more powerful case for public will to sweep the issue toward political will.

SOME SAY THIS IMPROVED status quo for women cannot last; that all it will take is a natural disaster like an earthquake, a tsunami, a famine, or even an economic depression for the gains made by women to come undone. I disagree. I believe the emancipation movement is beyond that. In fact, the disruption itself — the social disruption that calls out the old boys' club, the economic disruption that demands fair pay, and the political disruption that sees more women running for office than ever before — is reordering the way we live our lives. And that's the formula that created this power shift.

CHAPTER FIVE

SHIFTING POWER

IN JANUARY 2019, TUCKER CARLSON, a middle-aged host on America's Fox News, proclaimed, "Study after study has shown that when men make less than women, women generally don't want to marry them. Maybe they should want to marry them, but they don't. Over big populations this causes a drop in marriage, a spike in out-of-wedlock births, and all the familiar disasters that inevitably follow. More drug and alcohol abuse, higher incarceration rates, fewer families formed in the next generation. This is not speculation, it's not propaganda from the evangelicals. It's social science." Really?

What is it about men like Tucker Carlson that makes them want to say women don't belong here — in the workforce, the C-suite, the boardroom?

Janet Yellen, who became the first woman to head the U.S. Federal Reserve and is president-elect of the American Economic Association, says issues like this need to be the highest priority for economists in the years to come.

She was responding to a comment by Ben Bernanke, the president of the American Economic Association and former chair of the U.S. Federal Reserve, who said, "Economics certainly has a problem. The profession has unfortunately a reputation for hostility toward women and minorities." But women economists are fighting for change and seeking a #MeToo revolution in the industry. In 2019, many young economists and graduate students who belonged to the American Economic Association wrote an open letter to the administration, calling for codes of conduct to cope with the flagrant sexual harassment, enforcement of those codes of conduct, and an overhaul of the systems for reporting abuse. They wrote, "We shouldn't have to rely on whisper networks to protect us from abuse and inappropriate behaviour. And we don't have the power to discipline our supervisors or even our peers. You do. Please listen to us."

They could begin with some hard facts: white women are paid 79 cents for every dollar a white man makes. Black women earn only 63 cents on that dollar, Latinas just 54 cents. Asian women are paid the most — or, put another way, their wage gap is the least offensive — at 87 cents on the dollar. The wage gap for mothers is approximately 71 cents for every dollar paid to fathers.

In 2018, SmartAsset, a U.S. financial company, analyzed Bureau of Labor Statistics data to ascertain the largest and smallest gender pay gaps by occupation. Not surprisingly, financial adviser was the job with the largest gap. Of the ten biggest gaps, four are in the finance sector, which still employs far more men than women. But even in real estate, in which the majority of brokers are female, women earn only 70.5 percent of what their male counterparts make. The smallest gaps are found among licensed practical nurses, wholesale and retail buyers, and counsellors. In fact, counselling was the only job out of the 121 analyzed that showed women earning more money than men.

According to this data, even the professions can't close the wage gap: women doctors earn 63 percent of what is earned by their male colleagues. Wage gaps cost the economy — trillions of dollars, in the case of the U.S. And to compound the problem, it'll cost more as women retire having saved less money for retirement, and therefore having less to add to the economy.

The U.K. has commissioned similar gender pay studies for any company with more than 215 employees. The reports, released in 2018, show women are clustered at the bottom. There is a great deal of variation across sectors. As in the U.S., finance is the worst: some financial and insurance companies report a gap of 35.6 percent; for 1.5 percent of firms, the gap is at 50 percent. But the problem reaches well beyond the financial district. As one example, even the female staff at Buckingham Palace are paid a mean of 12 percent less than the male staff, and the discrimination even extends to the palace's TV counterpart: actor Claire Foy, who had the starring role playing Queen Elizabeth II in the Netflix series *The Crown*, made less than Matt Smith, who played the supporting character Prince Philip.

There are consequences to sidelining women. Unlike the "studies" Mr. Carlson refers to, a vast number of studies show that if women are at the table (the boardroom table, the political table, the community table) the economy will improve. *The Economist* reports that the increase in the employment of women in developed countries during the past decade has added more to the global GDP than

China has. If India, the world's biggest democracy, introduced gender balance to its workforce, it would be 27 percent richer. If women farmers had the same quality seeds, fertilizer, and tools as men farmers, they could feed 150 million more people worldwide. What's more, poverty and conflict would abate.

In 2004, I came face to face with a heartbreaking and infuriating example of a family condemned to poverty, when I met a woman called Gowramma in a village called Etangur, outside of Bangalore in southern India. Gowramma is a Dalit, a Sanskrit word that means "broken people," formerly known as untouchables (today the caste is known, less offensively, as the "scheduled caste"). Her story struck me because she knows exactly how to get herself out of the enforced poverty she and her husband and three children live with. They use cheap cereal grains for food and they are not allowed to access fresh water, because the well is across the line that divides the scheduled caste from the others. They wait until the well on their side of the road is turned on — sometimes for three days. But Gowramma has a plan. She owns two cows. She wants to start a dairy and says she could provide milk to the people in the village, enough milk to earn the money to get her husband out of bondage, enough to have better-quality food for her children. But the upper castes in India won't allow her to do that. It's a rule that affects 200 million members of the scheduled caste; that's 20 percent of the population in India. Changing the rule would not only improve the lives of Gowramma and her family, it would contribute to solving the food shortage in the region where they live.

Muhammad Yunus, the Bangladeshi banker, economist, and founder of the Grameen Bank, found the same thing when he befriended a group of women weavers on the streets of Dhaka near the bank where he worked. He discovered the women were paying a lender usurious fees for the cash they needed to buy their bamboo, and worse, they were selling their finished products back to the lender, who was grossly underpaying them. Yunus thought the bank where he was employed could help them out with loans at the going rate. The bank was outraged at the suggestion of lending money to poor people. So Yunus opened his own bank and discovered that the women paid him back in total and on time. His conclusion? "Poverty is unnecessary."

Systems in place all over the world deny fair wages and sideline women earners. At the World

Economic Forum in Davos, Switzerland, in January 2017, Michael Cole-Fontayn, executive vice-president and chairman of Europe, Middle East, and Africa for BNY Mellon, said, "We not only have a moral imperative to bridge the global gender gap, but the potential market benefits and investment opportunities in doing so are pivotal. Companies engaging in 'gender-lens' investing have typically supported women-led businesses and those promoting gender diversity. However, there is an increasing need to focus on the third (and less common) type of investing, in companies that advance gender equality through their products and services."

So why is the economics sector a no-fly zone for so many women? As it turns out, it has more to do with the attitudes of men than the education of women. In *The Moment of Lift*, a book that is part life story and part call to action for women's empowerment, the American philanthropist Melinda Gates questions the underlying assumptions. She quotes a friend and co-worker who said, "It's not okay for women to cry at work, but it's okay for men to YELL at work." And she questions the attitude that courtesy is a sign of weakness.

"We're quick to criticize gender injustice when we

see it around the world. We also need to see it where most of us feel it and can do something about it — in the places where we work," she says. "We're sending our daughters into a workplace that was designed for our dad — set up on the assumption that employees had partners who would stay at home to do the unpaid work of caring for the family."

One of the ways to change the workplace is for women to exert more power in the financial sector, whether they are part of a pension plan, as most workers are, or dealing with the C-suite. "If women get together as spenders, consumers, shareholders, they could change the world," says Toronto financial wizard Dona Eull-Schultz. "Do the basic math: what percentage of the world is female? How many assets are controlled by women? Now look at the population numbers — who owns the assets in the thirty-to-forty age group, in the forty-to-fifty, in the fifty-to-sixty and above? The math tells you women live longer and own most of the assets. That's power." Eull-Schultz emphasizes that "if you have a retirement plan, if you have an RSP or any kind of investment, you are a shareholder, an owner in a company. That means you get to vote on board decisions. You have the right to ask questions, such as, 'What is your policy about equal pay for work of equal value; how many women do you have on your board of directors; what's your protocol on sexual harassment in the workplace; what is your plan for hiring women?' They are obliged to answer your questions. Put your wallet where your values are."

This is more than just a question of fairness. Underutilizing women's talent is enormously costly in an economy afflicted by low productivity growth and skill shortages. In 2018, California passed a law that fines a company $100,000 if its board of directors includes no women. The second time, it's a $300,000 fine. A lot of countries in the European Union have quotas for women on boards. In 2019, the Law Society of Ontario conducted a full ranking of men to women, forcing firms to make statements about diversity. Camilla Sutton, president and CEO of Women in Capital Markets, says that we know very well that we need diversity for companies to be successful, "so now is the time for more awareness and education and a means of managing inclusivity without bias." In two decades, the presence of women in capital markets has moved at a snail's pace, from 10 percent to 13 percent. Out of 312 executive officers in Canada, only 24 are women. In fact, Canada is near the bottom in almost every measure of women in capital markets in the developed world.

The tech sector also needs to "mind the gap." The president of IBM Canada, Ayman Antoun, writes this: "The Canadian tech sector has never been stronger, with job growth in Toronto outpacing Silicon Valley, and tech-related employment growing four times faster than overall employment in Canada. This growth is having a positive impact on our economy, but it has also resulted in a vacuum of skilled resources that are needed to keep pace. Why is it, then, that women only represent just over 27 percent of the Canadian information and communications technology work force? A number that has not changed much over the years and has actually declined from a high of 29 percent in 2011." He's referring to the fact that women and girls have not usually engaged in technology, and that, he suggests, is a large untapped pool of talent. No wonder STEM — science, technology, engineering, and math — is the new panacea in high school curriculums today. The teachers and professors and Antoun himself claim this is the opening girls need because this is where the jobs are going to be — the jobs that offer faster promotion and higher income and drive the economy. Antoun feels that girls need to be trained now in STEM programs engaged with technology-building skills that lead to related careers, or they'll be left behind.

In fact, one study claims there's a $92-billion annual economic cost to undereducating girls relative to boys. And according to the International Monetary Fund, improved gender equality at work would increase the GDP of the U.S. by 5 percent, of Japan by 9 percent, and of Egypt by 34 percent.

Today, women constitute 40 percent of the labour force and 43 percent of the agricultural workforce; more of us are part of the formal paid workforce than ever before. In 2013, the accountancy firm Grant Thornton conducted a global survey and found that women fill 24 percent of senior management roles — and, slowly, that percentage is rising. But, writes Nikki van der Gaag, in her 2014 book *Feminism and Men*:

> Women make up only 16 percent of board members in the rich-world G7 economies compared with 26 percent in the BRIC economies (Brazil, Russia, India and China) and 38 percent in the Baltic countries ... This means that in Japan, 93 out of every 100 people in top positions are men, in the USA this is 80

out of 100, and even in the countries at the top of the list, only China has more women than men, and this is a leap from 25 per cent the previous year. And interestingly, despite many years of legislation for gender equality, Sweden and Norway are only 27 and 22 in the ranking of top countries.

As much as closing the wage gap is frustratingly slow, the power of women's voices is being felt elsewhere, with trend-changing consequences. In 2019, Secretary-General António Guterres appointed women leaders in every regional economic sector of the UN — Western Asia, Latin America and the Caribbean, Asia and the Pacific, Europe, and Africa. Although the sectors have been in position for seventy years, this is the first time ever that each one is headed by a woman. And at the 2019 Grammy Awards the show opened with five powerful women — Lady Gaga, Michelle Obama, Jada Pinkett Smith, Alicia Keyes, and Jennifer Lopez — talking about the role of music in their lives. The message was louder than that: we're women — pay attention, times are changing.

Frances McDormand's Best Actress acceptance speech at the 2018 Oscars demanded "inclusion riders," which means 50 percent of jobs — the actors and directors, the camera and sound technicians — are filled by women. Although few stars have been willing to publicly support the idea, it's out there now for discussion. Geena Davis started this concept in 2002. After playing Thelma in *Thelma and Louise* and then Dottie Hinson in *A League of Their Own*, she had realized that the way women are portrayed in the media is almost exactly the way they are treated in public. So she opened the Geena Davis Institute on Gender in the Media. She told me that she was doing what she could about being a changemaker. She said, "You can write about the women and girls around the world, but I work in this business; this is the part I can change." The first research she commissioned showed that 17 percent was the cut-off point for the acceptable number of women and girls in a film scene — more than that was considered "too many women." She says that now, "68 to 78 percent of the incoming students in forensic science at universities are female. And about 78 percent of the young actors playing forensic scientists on TV are women." She takes that as a win and adds, "If they can see it, they can be it."

Tackling change in the workplace is a perilous

task. The obstacles are mostly what Canadian psychologist and lawyer Delee Fromm calls "gender blind spots" — the beliefs and habits and stereotypes we learn in childhood that steer the way we and others should behave based on gender. They have a significant impact on women's careers. One of those beliefs is that women do less well in maths and sciences and should gravitate toward education and the arts.

When the award-winning film *The Imitation Game* came out in 2014, it stunned audiences to learn that Alan Turing was persecuted for being gay, despite the fact that he helped Britain break German codes that led to winning the Second World War. But most moviegoers were equally stunned to learn that the majority of his team of code breakers and communication specialists were women. The work of these women had been shrouded in secrecy for seventy years. The 2016 film *Hidden Figures*, based on the bestselling non-fiction book by Margot Lee Shetterly, told the story of three Black women mathematicians who were the brains behind the launch of astronaut John Glenn into orbit in 1962. But as the movie depicts, they were dealing with overt racism and segregation, even being required to leave their posts and

run to another building to use the washroom desig-
nated for Black women. While Glenn's story played
in the headlines for decades, the splendid work
and success of these brilliant women were hardly
known until the twenty-first century.

Both films play into Fromm's theory about gender gaps. She says there are four key elements to
look out for: the first are the things we learned from
the playground to the classroom to the boardroom;
second, the rules we use to socialize and commu-
nicate; third, the way we interact; and finally, the
way we lead and behave based on rules that are fun-
damentally different. Boys are taught to stand out;
in direct contrast, girls learn that fitting in is crucial — relationships being paramount. Power among
girls is equal and shared, while among boys it is
hierarchical. The women at NASA assumed their
work would go unrecognized.

Women also need to consider the way they
make their value visible. Since most leaders today
are men, and the history of paid work has been
predominately male, the modus operandi of men
becomes the operating code at work. Most women,
who have long played by "feminine" rules such as
sharing and caring, are at a significant disadvan-
tage. Doing excellent work alone in your office day

after day is not enough, says Fromm. You have to tell people about it. As for closing the wage gap, women know very well that they are better than men at negotiating on behalf of others — just ask the women in the office who wanted better washroom facilities and took up the task of getting them. Or ask a child who was shunned in the park — who dealt with the bully? But women do not do well when negotiating for themselves; we know that to be true.

Not asking for or negotiating a higher salary is a gender blind spot, says Fromm. She points out two reasons why women refrain from asking: fear of the relationship being damaged and the resulting diminished reputational cost, and "lack of knowledge about what, how and when to negotiate." Finally, she says, if women adopt a traditionally male style of leadership, "they risk being judged as hostile, strident, masculine, demanding or domineering, not to mention unlikeable." If they adhere to a more traditionally feminine approach, they are seen as more likeable but are "judged as not tough enough, too accommodating and not competent," even though the research has shown that leadership styles that are most effective are those associated with feminine approaches.

While the male-driven land of economics and success is still one of the last bastions of gender exclusion, women throughout history have masqueraded as men to find ways to reach their own goals: to become composers (Fanny Mendelssohn), writers (the Brontë sisters), students (the girls of Afghanistan). Others disguised themselves so they could go to war, like Elisa Bernerström, who joined the Swedish army in 1808. Mary Ann Evans published six books in the latter half of the nineteenth century as George Eliot. Kathrine Switzer entered the Boston marathon in 1967 as K. V. Switzer because women were not allowed to run in the race; when she was spotted and identified as a woman, one of the race directors demanded she leave the course and tried to rip the number off her shirt. Even J. K. Rowling chose her pen name in 1997 so her gender would be less obvious than if she'd used her proper name, Joanne Rowling. And when she penned her adult novels, she used the pseudonym Robert Galbraith. But one of the most bizarre stories of commitment and determination comes from St. Marina. As a child in the eighth century, she disguised herself as a boy so she could visit a monastery with her father — women were barred. She grew up to be a monk herself and went by the name Marinus. Incredibly, after an innkeeper's daughter claimed Marinus had impregnated her and Marina was kicked out of the monastery, she raised the child herself rather than revealing her secret and therefore the absurdity of the charge. The truth came out posthumously, and the Coptic Orthodox Church made her a saint.

Even making their true identity known didn't spare women from being misrepresented. There's a story oft told by the University of Toronto political scientist and author Sylvia Bashevkin about the first day Agnes Macphail entered the House of Commons in the early 1920s, representing the Progressive Party. She'd been elected a scant few years after women won the right to vote. Instead of heralding the issues she brought to Parliament, the newspapers of the day described Miss Macphail as dressed in a wide-brimmed pale blue chapeau and a fetching dress to match: "Macphail's entry to Parliament was headline news in the social pages of the nation's newspapers, which devoted considerable attention to her hat, gloves, and dress. All were found wanting, as severe, worn out, unfashionable, and downright dowdy." Macphail's words in the House of Commons were slightly less docile:

"When I hear men talk about being the angel of the home I always, mentally at least, shrug my shoulders in doubt. I do not want to be the angel of any home; I want for myself what I want for other women, absolute equality. After that is secured then men and women can take turns at being angels."

The fallout of equality hasn't always been angelic. The fact that two-thirds of women in European parliaments experience sexual harassment is another worrisome sign of the times. While the power is shifting toward inclusiveness for women, a backlash from men reminds us that if we are to reach our goal of equality, we need to walk together. Let me explain.

In 2019, I was asked to be part of a panel discussion at the Harvard Kennedy School on the online sexual harassment of women journalists. I began my brief address by sharing a story with the audience to illustrate the point that there is nothing new about the harassment of public figures; only the style and official response have altered. I went on to tell them I was a cub reporter in the 1980s when I received my first death threat. It arrived with the daily mail, delivered by a friendly man who hauled grey mailbags to our editorial offices each morning at about eleven a.m. The letter was in an envelope duly stamped and addressed to me. I am presuming it came from a man, but I don't have proof of that; however, I continued my story as though it was a man. He had carefully protected his anonymity by cutting out words from the recent edition of the magazine where I worked at the time, *Canadian Living*. He'd assembled the cut-out words in sentences that described the way he was going to kill me. The words were taken from the recipe section of the magazine. They read, "Cut breast in half; remove skin, pound until flat." It was a pretty gruesome letter. Naturally, I passed it around to my colleagues, and just as naturally, my editor at the time called the police. We just presumed the author of the letter was a crackpot and the police would take care of everything. In fact, the police did come to the editorial offices, plopped the offending letter into a plastic bag, and left after asking me what I had done to warrant such a letter. Later they called to ask if I had shown the letter to anyone else. I said that I had. They asked how many people had touched the letter. I had to admit it had been passed around to at least fifty people. Well, they said, they were trying to collect fingerprints. I promised that in future I would simply read the threat to my colleagues and hopefully preserve the prints. That was then.

My career writing about women and girls in conflict zones subsequently attracted other people who didn't approve of what I wrote, so the death threats didn't end, but they did change. In the nineties, they came by way of telephone calls at *Homemaker's*. I had a wonderful executive assistant, Shiraz Bagli, who used to entertain anyone around her desk when such a threat came in. She would simply call across the hall to my office and say, "Sally, death threat, line two." Because there was a real voice attached to the call, the threat was more disturbing. Listening to a man describe the serrated edge of the knife he was going to use to cut my throat certainly caught my attention. But I used to think threats coming from war zones were somehow about the anger of the caller more than the action he might take. Of course I would hang up, but my point is, we didn't have the technology in those days to prevent the call or even to identify the caller. Now we do.

Now with caller ID and all the technology to stop such horrible calls, and laws that describe them as crimes, the online harassment of women journalists has turned into an art form. There's hardly a woman journalist out there who has not been on the receiving end of frightening, intimidating, scurrilous, and bothersome harassment. Why? Because it is not seen as a big enough problem to be worth the action required to stop it. It's the same sidelining of women that we have known for ten thousand years. The most common accusation we get from the trolls is "lying whore" (or "stupid whore" or "fake-news whore"). The most common threat is "I will rape you"—with descriptions that aren't fit for print but somehow make it online. I find it very hard to fathom why Facebook, Google, and all the other online sites cannot find a way to put an end to this illegal, revolting behaviour that encourages online trolls to pump up their fury.

There's a memorable story out of Toronto in which a troll targeted a female sports reporter at a soccer game with the oft-repeated meme "Fuck her right in the pussy." When a group of male bystanders admitted they'd been planning to say the same thing, CityNews reporter Shauna Hunt challenged them while the camera continued to roll. "It's a disgusting thing to say. It's degrading to women," she said. "I don't care, it's fucking hilarious," one man answered. "You would humiliate me on live television?" she asked another. "I'm sick of it. I get this every single day. Ten times a day by rude guys like you." The man mocked her, dipping his face into her mic to imitate her words: *"I'm sick of it."*

The video went viral. As it turns out, the man who claimed the meme is "hilarious" was an assistant management engineer earning $106,000 a year in his job with Hydro One, the energy provider for Ontario. He was promptly fired for violating the company code of conduct. But he filed a grievance with his union, and after arbitration, Shawn Simoes got his job back.

While this wasn't an online attack, it does prove that even visible harassment of women journalists is a serious problem. In a study by Troll Busters and the International Women's Media Foundation, 40 percent of women journalists interviewed said they'd shelved stories that would attract attacks. About 30 percent admitted online abuse had prompted them to consider changing jobs altogether. After being subjected to online harassment, some women have also been attacked offline.

This is incredibly restricting. Women being forced to avoid online political debates is a level of censorship sensible people don't want. A 2018 European Institute for Gender Equality survey showed that slightly more than 50 percent of young women and 42 percent of young men have become hesitant to participate in social media debates because of online hate speech or abuse. The International Federation of Journalists (IFJ) did a global survey of women journalists that shows serious impacts of online abuse, affecting two-thirds of its members and taking such forms as death and rape threats, personal and professional insults, sexist comments, and obscene images. Forty-seven percent of the women who suffered harassment said that they did not report it. Sixty-three percent of abused respondents reported psychological effects, including anxiety and stress; 38 percent had self-censored; 8 percent had quit their jobs. The co-chair of IFJ's Gender Council, Mindy Ran, said, "This survey highlights one of the fastest growing forms of gender-based violence against women journalists as digital platforms encourage ease, impunity, and anonymity of aggression — the bastion of a coward and a bully hiding in plain sight. This survey . . . highlights the huge disconnect between experience and action, the lack of support mechanisms, unclear laws, and failure to fully implement those international treaties and labour standards that do exist. It is clear, we are failing to protect our sisters and the lack of recognition of the serious crime must be addressed at every level now." Even more disturbing, the women say their own colleagues don't take notice of the harassment of female journalists. They feel alone and without the support they deserve.

Carolyn Bennett refers to a story her mentor Ursula Franklin, the late, great peace activist and professor emeritus at the University of Toronto, told her: "I went to see Ursula Franklin in the fall of 2014 during a nasty harassment crisis on the Hill [Parliament Hill]. I told her that a journalist had emailed all the women Members of Parliament, asking if we had ever been harassed. She said immediately: 'He is asking the wrong question. He should be asking the men if they have ever harassed, ever crossed the line with inappropriate behaviour.'"

It raises the question — why *do* boys and men do things like that? And what's being done to alter this sort of sexist behaviour? One answer comes from a high school in Maryland called Bethesda–Chevy Chase. When the girls got word in March 2019 of a list being circulated by the male students that ranked them on their looks from 5.5 to 9.4, they were furious. They wondered who was watching them, and felt violated and objectified by their supposed friends. Lists like this are nothing new to high schools, but this is the age of #MeToo, and the girls felt empowered to take action. When they went together to the administrator and demanded disciplinary action for the boys involved, the punishment turned out to be a one-day in-school detention. So the girls marched — forty of them — to the vice-principal's office during the lunch hour to say publicly, "We feel unsafe in this environment and we are tired of this toxicity." They wanted to know what the school would do to ensure their safety and security: "We should be able to learn in an environment without the constant presence of objectification and misogyny." That resulted in a meeting of all the boys and all the girls affected, demanding not only disciplinary action in response to the list but a school-wide reckoning of the toxic culture that allowed it to happen.

The boy who created the list, an eighteen-year-old senior in the International Baccalaureate Program, spoke before the group and apologized for the damage he had done. "It was quite intense, being so directly confronted in front of so many people for so long," the student recalled in an interview with the *Washington Post*, speaking anonymously. "When you have a culture where it's just normal to talk about that, I guess making a list about it doesn't seem like such a terrible thing to do, because you're just used to discussing it." He said he was grateful the girls had taken a stand. "It's just a different time and things really do need to change. This memory is not going to leave me anytime soon." From then until the end of the school term in June, the students continued to meet and talk about what needs to change and how the changes can be made.

Another answer comes from Deloitte, the consulting and accounting firm that recently prepared a position paper called "The Design of Everyday Men: A New Lens for Gender Equality Progress." Since research has shown that inclusive business cultures outperform all others in terms of financial performance and innovation, the paper focused on balancing the new roles for men in the workplace, and how to cope with backlash when others think a man has stepped outside the traditional masculine gender norms. Many young men today play much more inclusive roles at home than their fathers did, but their role models at work still revolve around being "always on and always available" and the notion that more hours at work means more success. The evidence is to the contrary — more hours leads to poorer out-comes — but traditional masculinity keeps men tied to these expectations.

This conversation is being written into policies at the workplace and in government offices. The discussion among men in reaction to #MeToo is sometimes frivolous ("Enough is enough"), some-times wasteful ("Stay away from the women lest you be accused of assault"), and sometimes heart-felt, the same way women in the Sixties came to eye-opening conclusions after consciousness-raising conversations about their gender-prescribed roles. Many men feel they are hearing a woman's story for the first time. They are discovering that liberating women also liberates men, that gender equality works both ways. This shift in power is crucial to our collective thriving.

As much as anti-women views are politically incorrect today, questions linger:

- How can a corporation or anyone else pay a woman less money for doing the same job a man is doing? Is greed so rampant and profit so paramount that people don't count?
- How can men harm their wives and daugh-ters and claim their actions are God's will?

Or beat them up and blame it on rage — or, worse, the victims?

- Who is the person who decided that giving young girls virginity tests is a policy that leads to goodness?
- What are men afraid of when they refuse to send girls to school, where they can learn to think for themselves?
- Why would a man rape a woman? Is there no other way he can express his anger or his insatiable need for power and control?

As the power shifts, men who care about their mothers and wives, sisters, and daughters are taking up the quarrel women have with the foes of equality.

I remember giving a speech in a large downtown church in Toronto about women and the violence perpetrated against them. The place was packed. There was a question period afterwards, and the minister of the church asked a question that stunned me: "What can the Church do about this?" I was flabbergasted by his colossal naivety and replied as gently as I could that if he stood in his pulpit on Sunday mornings and preached that violence against women is a sin in the eyes of God, it would go a long way to starting a conversation with men that desperately needs to begin. And I suggested he say that anyone listening should know that such behaviour is abhorrent, and that help is available to people with tempers that flare out of control and lead to physical, verbal, and sexual assault, and that he could provide a number for them to call and a promise of anonymity.

For all the changes in the status of women and all the progress made for our daughters, the outlier that acts as the last bastion of the old guard, the one that stubbornly resists change, is the dark and secret underbelly of intimate partner violence. It simply must stop. Its consequences cost billions of dollars. Its scars are everlasting. And it has a way of injecting itself into the next generation. But it will not stop until men are part of the conversation.

I'm often asked why my journalistic work concentrates on girls. With all this pressure to advance girls, what's to become of the boys? they ask.

That question always brings me back to a story I covered in Somalia during the civil war in 1993. I was following a shipment of wheat to find out what exactly happened to it along the way. The centre of the famine belt was a place called Baidoa. I travelled there by night from the capital, Mogadishu, to avoid the unrest in the towns and the strife on the road. Somalis chew a leafy green plant called khat, which first acts as a stimulant and then leads to numbness and lack of concentration. So a midnight departure from Mogadishu seemed like a prudent idea, since most of the troublemakers would have fallen asleep by late evening. Baidoa was crowded with people seeking relief and with humanitarian agencies serving them.

But the story I want to share happened at the therapeutic feeding centre, which is pretty much the end of the line in the famine business. Most who come here are very sick with famine-related diseases, close to death. All manner of emergency means are used to save them — intravenous feeding, high-protein biscuits, and Unimix, a high-protein porridge. On my way into the feeding centre I stood to one side and watched a man carrying a dead child wrapped in a tarp. Once inside, I first noticed how dark and damp the place was — a cement building, damaged by rockets but surprisingly cold given the scorching Somali sun outside.

Then I noticed a little child lying on a straw mat. He looked for all the world like a bag of bones. He was lying there as still as the air. I asked the woman in charge, an aid worker with the Irish branch of a non-governmental organization called Caritas, what had happened to the child? This is the story she told me.

He lived with his mother and father and five other siblings in a village a two-day walk from Baidoa. He was six years old, although to me he looked three — when children are starving, they tend to look half their age; when adults are starving, they tend to look twice their age. She told me that this child's father had argued with the warlord in charge of his village about the lack of food for his family, and was shot dead. The mother was already being deprived of the donated food coming into the villages via convoys, such as the one I had hitched a lift with the night before. Her strength was compromised, but she had to make a decision — stay and die from starvation, or leave with the six children and hope she could make it to Baidoa and find help in time. Four of the children died along the way. Just imagine that. What was she to do with them, where could she bury them? She hardly had the strength to walk. She left her four children, one at a time, by the side of the road and carried on with the two survivors. They made it to Baidoa and were directed by others to the therapeutic feeding centre. The next day, the mother and another one of

her children died. This little boy was the sole sur-
viving member of that family.

I wanted to tell his story; I also wanted to take
his photo. There was no parent to ask for permission, so I turned to the matron, and she said
it would be all right. I kneeled at the end of the
mat he was lying on and positioned my camera. I
turned on the flash, as it was dark in the room. He
lay there, unaware. But when the flash went off on
my camera, this little child began to stir, looking
for the source of the light. I thought to myself, *My
God, he's so sick, but he still has that wonderful curi-
osity we adore in children.* Then his scrawny little
neck moved far enough around that he saw me at
the end of his mat. A giant woman with yellow hair.
So there we were — our eyes made contact. What
do you do when you make eye contact with a child?
You smile, right? I smiled at this boy, all the while
thinking what hopelessly inappropriate behaviour
this was, to be smiling at a child who was so terri-
bly ill. But here's the thing. He smiled back at me.
He was almost dead, this poor little boy, but he
still wanted to make friends with a total stranger.

His story has never left me. His little face and
huge eyes play on the back of my eyelids whenever I wonder how it is that affable little kids — girls

and boys from North America, Europe, Asia, and Africa — grow up to be teachers or warlords, doctors or rapists, soccer players or suicide bombers. What happens along the way to influence each of us?

Shifting power is about women and girls walking beside the men and boys. It's time for the men to speak up and walk with the women. And it's time for women to disrupt old mores. History has known outspoken radicals who were dismissed for being impractical or dangerous but whom modern society now extols. They include well-known women like Rosa Parks and Canadian civil rights trailblazer Viola Desmond, the Black woman from Halifax who refused to bow to white rule and sat in the whites-only section of a movie theatre and was arrested and dragged out of the theatre. Today her photo graces the Canadian ten-dollar bill. Doria Shafik challenged cultural, legal, and social norms for women in Egypt in the mid-twentieth century and is credited with getting women the right to vote. Her work was buried and resurfaced only recently. And Nellie McClung, who was ridiculed when she fought for the vote for women and in 1915 famously said, "Never retract, never explain, never apologize — get the thing done and let them howl." And Doris Anderson of Canada, who, like Betty

Friedan of the U.S., called for women's liberation at a time when many thought that was frivolous.

When ideas shift from the fringes to the mainstream, they seem to rely on unpredictable circumstances, individuals, and events. One of the preconditions is widespread discontent and distrust of political, social, and economic structures. That's when new ideas catch on. And the internet acts as a speed dial for getting the information out. "Radicals don't always need to win to influence mainstream thinking," says author Jamie Bartlett. Which slides right into a woman's way of making change. Women tend to act rather than call for a policy paper. Women collaborate, make people feel valued. Loyalty is important. It's about instinct, people saying, "I thought so." And it's about working collaboratively — "Let's do this." This emphasis on networks over hierarchies and leadership sharing over top-down management has been embraced by the corporate world. And that is likely ground zero for change. New power doesn't hold to the old traditional leadership style; it relies instead on mass participation. It also relies on a frame of mind that says enough is enough, which is why #MeToo caught on so powerfully. Everyone could relate to it. The language spoke of inclusiveness and familiarity. There was no complicated interpretation.

Experts like Nikki van der Gaag say women need to stop relying on softly-softly approaches like lobbying, recrafting laws, and using good-news messages such as "Your company will earn more money if you have women on the board." Why not a more robust demand, like the one the women of Liberia made when they called a sex strike as part of their Mass Action for Peace — no sex until the men agreed to stop the civil war. On April 23, 2003, the tyrannical ruler Charles Taylor agreed to meet the women and their leader, Leymah Gbowee. More than two thousand women gathered outside his executive mansion. "We are tired of war," Gbowee told him. "We are tired of running. We are tired of begging for bulgur wheat. We are tired of our children being raped. We are now taking this stand, to secure the future of our children. Because we believe, as custodians of society, tomorrow our children will ask us, 'Mama, what was your role during the crisis?'" Her words and the sex strike she organized resulted in a ceasefire. Gbowee won the Nobel Peace Prize in 2011.

It's amazing, isn't it, that women and men are so different — in the way we see each other, in the way we act, react, think, and perform one to the other. What's new is that those differences have been documented now, examined with new tools such as positron emission tomography (PET) and functional magnetic resonance imaging (MRI) to see how the brain functions when it is solving problems, producing ideas, falling in love, and feeling depression, fear, anxiety. Now there's proof that there are structural, chemical, genetic, hormonal, and functional brain differences between men and women. Dr. Louann Brizendine, who captured this thinking in her book *The Female Brain*, says, "We've learned that men and women have different brain sensitivities to stress and conflict. They use different brain areas and circuits to solve problems, process language, experience and store the same strong emotion. Women may remember the smallest details of their first dates, and their biggest fights, while their husbands barely remember that these things happened. Brain structure and chemistry have everything to do with why this is so." One of the conclusions of this work is that "women are, on average, better at expressing emotions and remembering the details of emotional events. Men, by contrast, have two and a half times the brain space devoted to sexual drive as well as larger brain centres for action and aggression. Sexual thoughts float through a man's brain many times each day on average, and through a woman's only once a day."

We knew that, didn't we? We have lived it all our lives — both men and women. We read about it in the 1990s, when John Gray wrote his bestselling *Men Are from Mars, Women Are from Venus*. He wrote about the psychology of stress and conflict, claiming women and men act as though they come from different planets with different attitudes, cultures, and coping mechanisms. One of Gray's examples is that, faced with stress, men escape into their caves (a.k.a. the garage, the hockey rink) and women want to talk and talk and talk to deal with the stress. Now with the imaging work done on the brain, with Louann Brizendine's research fourteen years later, we know precisely that we are different one to the other. Microscopic brain analysis shows that women have 11 percent more neurons than men in the centres for language and hearing. The hippocampus — the hub of emotion and memory function — is larger in the female brain, which explains why women are better at expressing emotions and remembering details of emotional events.

Is that the missing data for taking women to the

finish line in the equality stakes? Maybe. It does tackle erroneous assumptions such as the long-held view that women aren't as good as men in math and science. In fact, the studies show males and females have the same average level of intelligence. They also show that as boys and girls hit their teen years, there is no difference in their scientific and mathematical capacity. But as estrogen floods the female mind, Louann Brizendine says, "Females start to focus intensely on their emotions and on communication — talking on the phone and connecting with their girlfriends at the mall. At the same time, as testosterone takes over the male brain, boys grow less communicative and become obsessed with scoring — in games, and in the backseat of a car . . . boys can easily retreat alone to their rooms for hours of computer time."

So we know — we're different. But how does that explain the violence, the sidelining, the oppression? Attacking the women who report the news, the sports, the weather, the markets is a sure sign that some male egos are running amuck. This is misogyny — the hatred of women. It's the same misogyny the Taliban showed during the five years the women of Afghanistan were made prisoners in their own homes. The world looked the other way until 9/11. It's the same misogyny ISIS displayed in the taking of five thousand Yazidi women and girls as sex slaves. It was four years before they were released. I think it's time to take action on trolls, on abusers of all sorts. Take Brunei, for example, a small and wealthy country in Southeast Asia on the island of Borneo that, in 2019, introduced a brutal set of punishments, including amputating limbs and lashes with a whip, for the so-called crimes of being gay, committing adultery, and speaking against Islam, also known as blasphemy. This is barbaric.

Then there's Afghanistan. After the international community invested billions of dollars setting up democratic institutions, building systems that create trust, and altering the status of women in Afghanistan, how could U.S. President Donald Trump throw away all the gains just to fulfill his vow to get out of Afghanistan? How could he decide to negotiate troop withdrawal with the Taliban, who dismiss the legitimate Afghan government, ignore the democratic institutions that have been created, and threaten the lives and livelihoods of women and girls?

Like the students at Bethesda–Chevy Chase High School, we need to invite the men to stand with us and to right the wrongs. It's time for the men to speak out and walk with the women. I call on bosses and jocks, preachers and teachers, politicians and dads, to put their truth to the test at the barricades. Your girlfriends and sisters and wives and mothers and daughters are waiting for you to turn up.

IT'S BEEN A LONG JOURNEY for women everywhere. We've come such a distance since prehistoric people enchanted their descendants with cave drawings 27,000 years ago. I began this lecture series wondering what those early artists had to teach us, especially since we've learned the drawings were done by women as well as men. But a longer explanation comes from archaeologist and writer Leslie Van Gelder, who specializes in cave art that tells us about women and children and intimacy and relationships. She also supervises Ph.D. students in education at Walden, an American online university.

Van Gelder, who is based in Glenorchy, New Zealand, is a world expert in finger flutings, which are the residue of a person's touch, the lines people during the Upper Paleolithic period drew with their hands on the walls and ceilings of caves found in France, Spain, and Australia.

She told her remarkable story in a TEDx Talk in Queenston, New Zealand, in 2015, and in doing so, enthralled her listeners with a meditation on relationship and intimacy. She brings the past closer to us as she reimagines the relationships between the people who blew ochre over their hands so that their imprints would be left on the walls of the caves. These Upper Paleolithic people were taller and thinner than we are; they didn't live in the caves, except maybe in the front chambers. She examined the drawings on the cave walls — the mammoths and bisons and rhinoceros, and something others have suggested was a form of graffiti or calligraphy — and measured the finger flutings to determine hand width. Her quest was to try to better understand who did all of this. She started looking for relationships, intimacies. Many were pairs — a mother fluting with her left hand, her child with his right hand — and there was a four-year-old girl whose flutings particularly enchanted Van Gelder.

"Twenty-seven thousand years ago," she says, "people blew ochre over their hands and left marks on the walls that are still visible today. My favourite among them is one that's unfortunately . . . faded. But it's the marks of an infant whose hand was held up . . . and the adult had blown . . . ochre over their hand and had also caught the wrist of the person who was holding them."

She delicately weaves the pieces of history together by interpreting the stories being told on these cave walls — layer upon layer of engravings "of horses and bison and deer and auroch, and even of a little bird tangled up in this morass of images." And she describes a walk through one cave: "There are four engravings around you. The first that you see are the marks made by a Roman centurion two thousand years ago. And then, to your left, you see a dagger that was drawn during the Neolithic, eight thousand years ago. There's a cross that was done by the Knights Templar, eight hundred years ago. And then there's a horse just next to you, drawn during the Upper Paleolithic, 27,000 years ago."

Her work is all about what she calls the "archaeology of intimacy." Like a mother holding her child's hand up to the cave wall as she blows ochre across it — an instant that has lasted 27,000 years. She feels that we study the past to make those same kinds of connections, "to reach our hand back and find it met." It's a powerful concept, particularly in terms of what we are learning now about the missing lives of women in the ancient past.

Van Gelder explored intricate and sprawling caverns that to this day display the art people left behind. She says, "There've been a whole series of theories as to why people did this [made cave art] — everything from hunting magic to totemic symbols to hallucinating shamans in the dark. But really, there's been an awful lot of 'I don't know' that's couched in a lot of language around ritual and religiosity. Personally, I like the 'I don't knows' . . . that's where all the good questions lie."

She began to study hands and discovered that people have unique hand widths. When the glass of the shower door gets fogged up, you can draw your fingers across it and leave the same sort of mark she sees in the caves. "Even though your hand may look like your mother's, you actually don't make the same mark that your mother makes." And she discovered that anyone with a hand width of thirty millimetres or smaller was no older than five. "For the first time ever, we could find children in the caves."

Van Gelder had presumed that these caves were

ritual sites, visited season after season by hundreds of people, time after time, over millennia. But now she found something else. "In this enormous cave, there were only eight people who had done the finger flutings. Eight." In other caves she found even fewer.

She describes her work as "looking for the evidence of the visible and invisible relationships, and the small but indelible marks of human kindness." What she found is that no panel was made by a single individual. It was not a lone shaman in the dark. Instead it was always at least two. "In Gargas, I had . . . a woman with a child on her hip, she's fluting with her left hand, he's fluting with his right. Or in Las Chimeneas, in Spain . . . above the most beautiful deer drawings in history, two people are sitting side by side on a tiny little ledge, one's fluting with their left hand, the other with their right, and they must be passing their lamp back and forth between them in the darkness. Or in Rouffignac cave, a three-metre-long panel of two or three people fluting softly, ending with two mammoths facing each other."

Her favourite finger-fluter is a little girl, four years old, in the Rouffignac cave in France. She describes the child's twenty-eight-millimetre hand

and the way she drew her hands upward and down-
ward, across and back to make her mark.

> Every time I would work on her marks, I
> would have to put my torch under my arm,
> because she flutes with two hands ... And
> then one day it [hit me]. Why can she flute
> with two hands? Who's holding her light?
> There's no evidence of fire on the floor in this
> cave, so there has to be somebody who's there
> who's invisible to the final mark she makes,
> but was visible to her. And that's the person
> I'm most interested [in] in my work. That's
> the person I actually want to see.
>> Because I think each of us, in our own
> way in the world, we make our marks. Some
> of them are big. Some of them are huge,
> colossal. And some are small, momentary,
> intimate ... I propose that if we were to study
> the past and the present through the lens of
> relationship and intimacy, we might find a
> far more hopeful understanding of human-
> ity. Because I think we'd find evidence for
> what was true in this cave. Which is that,
> for each of us as we make our mark in the
> world, it's because someone else holds our

light. Whether that was 20,000 years ago
or today.

That's the truism I believe is leading us to the
equality we seek. Who is holding your light — in
the boardroom, the classroom, the bedroom? By
sharing that light, we are, each of us and all of us,
happier, more prosperous. And like the cave paint-
ers, we're leaving a legacy that says, "Together we're
better." The struggle women have endured to regain
our rights, to be ourselves, to be treated and paid
and understood as men are treated and paid and
understood, has been epic. This is our time. Now
is our hour.

People often ask me why I do this — why I follow
the plight of women and girls in zones of conflict.
I usually say it's because I think there must be a
better chapter yet to write about their lives. But I
might also take a page out of the brilliant work of
Greek photographer Yannis Behrakis, who died at
the age of fifty-eight in 2019 after photographing
some of the most moving evidence of trauma in
conflict zones and countries in crisis. My mission
has been to tell the story, record my eyewitness
reports of what happened to women and girls when
the world looked the other way. I feel as Yannis did

when he said, "My mission is to make sure that nobody can say: 'I didn't know.'"

Here's what we know now: Man the Hunter is bogus. There's no evidence to show that a woman was not right there hunting beside him. Women's history is a flawed account: the ancient past was recorded mostly by men about men. In fact, for millions of years, men and women had equal status.

Then they didn't.

During the agriculture era, when food became plentiful and humans could focus on development rather than sheer survival, both women and men realized that the future depended on producing more labourers. Only women had the sexual reproductive capacity to deliver a child. So women were appropriated by men to produce the next generation, much as land was privatized and acquired by men. That was the birth of patriarchy and the subordination of women. That subordination heightened when religion was formalized, and it was institutionalized in the early legal codes.

It's taken ten thousand years and a million voices to right those wrongs. The power shift came from the goddesses, priestesses, seers, diviners, nuns, healers, writers, reformers, activists, suffragettes, and feminists who took on the prophets and kings, the orators and philosophers, the politicians and bullies, to find justice, fairness, and equality for all. It's been history's longest revolution.

NOTES

CHAPTER 1: IN THE BEGINNING(S)

On the waves of feminism: Constance Grady, "The Waves of Feminism and Why People Keep Fighting over Them, Explained," *Vox*, July 20, 2018, https://www.vox.com/2018/3/20/16955588/feminism-waves-explained-first-second-third-fourth.

On new vs. old power: Jeremy Heimans and Henry Timms, *New Power: How Power Works in Our Hyperconnected World — and How to Make It Work for You* (Toronto: Random House, 2018), 2.

On pregnant students vanishing from campus: Anne Petrie, *Gone to an Aunt's: Remembering Canada's Homes for Unwed Mothers* (Toronto: McClelland & Stewart, 1998).

Geneva Conventions, paragraph 2, Article 7 of the Fourth Convention: https://ihl-databases.icrc.org/ihl/385ec082b509e76c41256739003e636d/6756482d86146898c125641e004aa3c5.

On *Newsweek*'s four-line report about soldiers gang-raping in the Balkans: Sally Armstrong, *Ascent of Women* (Toronto: Random House Canada, 2013), 40.

Gerda Lerner on the marginalization of women in historical scholarship: Gerda Lerner, *The Creation of Patriarchy* (New York: Oxford University Press, 1986), 4.

On archaeology's basis in male assumptions: Margaret W. Conkey and Janet D. Spector, "Archaeology and the Study of Gender," *Advances in Archaeological Method and Theory*, vol. 7 (Orlando, FL: Academic Press, 1984), 1–38, https://www.jstor.org/stable/20170176.

Amanda Foreman quote: *The Ascent of Woman*, episode 1, "Civilisation," directed by Hugo Macgregor, written and presented by Amanda Foreman, aired November 29, 2015, on BBC.

On the cost of violence against women: Lakshmi Puri, remarks delivered at the UN Economic Cost of Violence against Women discussion, September 21, 2016, http://www.unwomen.org/en/news/stories/2016/9/speech-by-lakshmi-puri-on-economic-costs-of-violence-against-women.

On the discovery of women's handprints on cave walls: Virginia Hughes, "Were the First Artists Mostly Women?," *National Geographic*, October 9, 2013, https://news.nationalgeographic.com/news/2013/10/131008-women-handprints-oldest-neolithic-cave-art/.

Christopher Muscato on prehistoric communal parenting: Christopher Muscato, "Roles of Women in the Stone Age," chapter 18, lesson 9, https://study.com/academy/lesson/roles-of-women-in-the-stone-age.html.

On the gender-egalitarian settlement at Çatalhöyük: Ian Hodder, "Women and Men at Çatalhöyük," *Scientific American*, January 1, 2005, https://www.scientificamerican.com/article/women-and-men-at-atalhyk-2005-01/?redirect=1; and "Çatalhöyük Excavations Reveal Gender Equality in Ancient Settled Life," October 2 , 2014, http://www.hurriyetdailynews.com/catalhoyuk-excavations-reveal-gender-equality-in-ancient-settled-life-72411.

On the Venus of Hohle Fels and similar figurines: April Nowell, "Paleo Porn," TEDx Talk, Victoria, BC, November 21, 2015, https://www.youtube.com/watch?v=ar92CdpowaY; interview with April Nowell, December 12, 2018; Nicholas J. Conard, "A Female Figurine from the Basal Aurignacian of Hohle Fels Cave in Southwestern Germany," *Nature*, May 14, 2009; Lewis Page, "Archaeologists

Unearth Oldest Known 3D Pornography," *The Register*, May 15, 2009, https://www.theregister.co.uk/2009/05/15/german_stone_a ge_3d_smut_figurine/.

On the role of women in the early agricultural era: Elise Boulding, *The Underside of History: A View of Women through Time* (Boulder, CO: Westview Press, 1976), cited in Lerner, *Patriarchy*, 43.

On the Sumerians' invention of the wheel, the plough, and writing: Megan Gambino, "A Salute to the Wheel," *Smithsonian Magazine*, June 17, 2009, https://www.smithsonianmag.com/science-nature/a-salute-to-the-wheel-31805121/; Autumn Stanley, *Mothers and Daughters of Invention: Notes for a Revised History of Technology* (New Brunswick, NJ: Rutgers University Press, 1995), 12; https://www.britishmuseum. org/explore/themes/writing/historic_writing.aspx.

On the original peoples of Nineveh: Ramy Jajo, "Who Are the Assyrians and What Are the Nineveh Plains?" *The Algemeiner*, September 19, 2014, https://www.algemeiner.com/2014/09/19/who-are-the-assyrians-and-what-are-the-nineveh-plains/.

On the role of women in Sumeria and the patriarchal laws of Assyria: Foreman, *The Ascent of Woman*, episode 1.

Cynthia Enloe on patriarchy: Cynthia Enloe, "The Persistence of Patriarchy," *New Internationalist*, October 1, 2017, https://newint. org/columns/essays/2017/10/01/patriarchy-persistence.

On the resistance to letting women drive in Saudi Arabia: Sebastian Usher, "'End of Virginity' If Women Drive, Saudi Cleric Warns," BBC, December, 2, 2011, https://www.bbc.com/news/ world-middle-east-16011926.

On women's rights in ancient Sparta vs. ancient Athens: William Richardson, "Women's Rights in Ancient Athens and Sparta," January 17, 2014, https://prezi.com/yaxnzxbrjfax/womens-rights-in-ancient-athens-and-sparta/.

On women's rights in ancient Egypt: Stacy Schiff, *Cleopatra: A Life* (New York: Little, Brown, 2010), 24.

On Confucianism in China: Xiongya Gao, "Women Existing for Men: Confucianism and Social Injustice against Women in China," *Race, Gender & Class* 10, no. 3 (2003), 114–25.

Confucian rules: http://www.womeninworldhistory.com/lesson3. html.

On the history of women in Japan: *The Ascent of Woman,* episode 2, "Separation," directed by Hugo Macgregor, written and presented by Amanda Foreman, aired December 6, 2015, on BBC.

On Caxton's printing of Christine de Pizan's *Faytes of Arms*: John Simkin, "Christine de Pizan: A Feminist Historian," Spartacus Educational, September 1997, updated July 2016, https://spartacus-educational.com/EXnormans15.htm.

On the percentage of women who were victims of witch trials: Robert Rapley, *A Case of Witchcraft: The Trial of Urbain Grandier* (Manchester, UK: Manchester University Press, 1998), 99.

On Catherine of Aragon and Henry VIII: Tim Lambert, "A Brief History of Women's Rights," revised 2019, http://www.localhistories. org/womensrights.html.

On Thomas Hobbes's views on women: *Stanford Encyclopedia of Philosophy,* s.v. "Hobbes's Moral and Political Philosophy," section 11, "Hobbes on Women and the Family," https://plato.stanford.edu/ entries/hobbes-moral/.

On Jean-Jacques Rousseau's views on women: Barbara Cattunar, "Gender Oppression in the Enlightenment Era," presented by Gillian Ellis at Humanist Society of New South Wales HuVAT meeting, July 13, 2014, http://hsnsw.asn.au/articles/WomenOfTheEnlightenment. pdf.

Olympe de Gouges's *Déclaration*: Olympe de Gouges, *The Declaration of the Rights of Women,* trans. Alayne Pullen (1791; reprint, Lewes, UK: Ilex Press, 2018).

On Marx's advocacy for industrial reforms: Micheline Ishay, introduction to chapter 8, "Challenging the Liberal Vision of Rights," *The Human Rights Reader: Major Political Essays, Speeches and Documents from Ancient Times to the Present,* 2nd ed. (New York: Routledge, 2007), 198.

John Stuart Mill's views on marriage: *Stanford Encyclopedia of Philosophy,* s.v. "John Stuart Mill," section 4.4, "Equality, the Sexes, and the Nineteenth Century," https://plato.stanford.edu/entries/mill/.

On coverture in the U.K.: Mary Lyndon Shanley, "Marital Slavery and Friendship: John Stuart Mill's *The Subjection of Women,*" *Political Theory* 9, no. 2 (May 1981), 229–47.

Reaction in Parliament to Mill's proposed amendment: Jamie Bartlett, *Radicals Chasing Utopia: Inside the Rogue Movements Trying to Change the World* (New York: Bold Type Books, 2017), 1.

Time's blurb on Emmeline Pankhurst: Marina Warner, "Time 100 People of the Century: Emmeline Pankhurst," *Time*, June 14, 1999.

Quote from the Covenant of the League of Nations: Article 23, Covenant of the League of Nations, the Avalon Project (Lillian Goldman Law Library, Yale Law School), https://avalon.law.yale.edu/20th_century/leagcov.asp.

On the UN adoption of the Universal Declaration of Human Rights: Sally Armstrong, "Missing in Access: A Feminist Critique of International Documents that Pertain to the Human Rights of Adolescent Girls to Access to Health Services and Their Impact on Young Women in Afghanistan and in Canada" (master's thesis, University of Toronto, 2001), 98, http://www.nlc-bnc.ca/obj/s4/f2/dsk3/ftp04/MQ63042.pdf.

On language in the Universal Declaration: Allida Black, "Are Women 'Human'? The UN and the Struggle to Recognize Human Rights as Women's Rights," in *The Human Rights Revolution: An International History* (New York: Oxford University Press, 2012), 139–41.

On Harvey Weinstein: Heimans and Timms, *New Power*, 2–3; Associated Press, "Weinstein's Sexual Assault Trial Delayed until December," *Los Angeles Times*, April 26, 2019, https://www.latimes.com/nation/nationnow/la-na-harvey-weinstein-trial-delayed-september-20190426-story.html; Ishani Nath, "The Disturbingly Long List of All the Women Who Have Accused Harvey Weinstein," *Flare*, November 13, 2017, https://www.flare.com/celebrity/harvey-weinstein-victims/.

Amnesty International's 2018 rights report: Amnesty International, *Rights Today: Why Our Movement Matters* (London: Amnesty International, 2018), 4, https://www.amnesty.ca/sites/amnesty/files/RightsTodayFINAL%20amend%2007%20Dec.pdf.

On the plight of girls worldwide: Sally Armstrong, *Veiled Threat: The Hidden Power of the Women of Afghanistan* (Toronto: Penguin, 2002), 84.

World Bank report on the consequences of inadequate education for girls: Quentin Wodon, Claudio Montenegro, Hoa Nguyen, and Adenike Onagoruwa, *Missed Opportunities: The High Cost of Not Educating Girls*, The Cost of Not Educating Girls Notes Series (Washington, DC: World Bank, 2018), https://openknowledge.worldbank.org/bitstream/handle/10986/29956/HighCostOfNotEducatingGirls.pdf.

Kristalina Georgieva on the gender education gap: Christina Rocca and Mark Ward, "Educate a Girl. Change the World," Central Asia Institute, https://centralasiainstitute.org/educate-a-girl-change-the-world/.

On Arturo Di Modica's objection to *Fearless Girl*: Associated Press, "'Charging Bull' Sculptor Says New York's 'Fearless Girl' Statue Violates His Rights," *The Guardian*, April 12, 2017, https://www.theguardian.com/us-news/2017/apr/12/charging-bull-new-york-fearless-girl-statue-copyright-claim; "A Full-on Art Fight Is Brewing on Wall Street after Artist Installs Peeing Dog Statue Next to *Fearless Girl*," *Vulture*, May 30, 2017, https://www.vulture.com/2017/05/artist-protests-fearless-girl-with-urinating-dog-sculpture.html.

On the removal of *Fearless Girl*: Ruben Kimmelman, "Gone Girl: Lower Manhattan 'Fearless Girl' Statue Is 'On the Move,'" NPR, November 28, 2018, https://www.npr.org/2018/11/28/671546407/gone-girl-lower-manhattan-fearless-girl-statue-is-on-the-move; "Mayor Announces New Home for 'Fearless Girl' Statue," Mayor's Office, New York City, April 19, 2018, https://www1.nyc.gov/office-of-the-mayor/news/202-18/mayor-de-blasio-new-home-fearless-girl-statue.

On the Department of Labor findings regarding State Street: Camila Domonoske, "Firm Behind 'Fearless Girl' Statue Underpaid Female, Black Execs, U.S. Says," NPR, October 6, 2017, ttps://www.npr.org/sections/thetwo-way/2017/10/06/556058808/firm-behind-fearless-girl-statue-underpaid-female-black-execs-u-s-says.

One in three women has experienced abuse: "Violence Against Women: Key Facts," World Health Organization, November 29, 2017, https://www.who.int/news-room/fact-sheets/detail/violence-against-women.

Statistics on genital mutilation: "Female Genital Mutilation: Key Facts," World Health Organization, January 31, 2018, https://www.who.int/news-room/fact-sheets/detail/female-genital-mutilation.

Statistics on human trafficking: *Global Report on Trafficking in Persons* (Vienna: United Nations Office on Drugs and Crime, 2018), 10, 28, https://www.unodc.org/documents/data-and-analysis/glotip/2018/GLOTiP_2018_BOOK_web_small.pdf.

Cost of intimate partner violence: Anke Hoeffler and James Fearon, "Post-2015 Consensus: Conflict and Violence Assessment," Copenhagen Consensus Center, 2014, https://www.copenhagenconsensus.com/publication/post-2015-consensus-conflict-and-violence-assessment-hoeffler-fearon.

Labour force participation rates: "The Gender Gap in Employment: What's Holding Women Back?," International Labour Organization, December 2017, updated March 2018, https://www.ilo.org/infostories/en-GB/Stories/Employment/barriers-women#intro.

Statistics on women's lack of access to certain jobs: "Facts and Figures: Economic Empowerment — Benefits of Economic Empowerment," UN Women, updated July 2018, http://www.unwomen.org/en/what-we-do/economic-empowerment/facts-and-figures.

On government support for oppressive policies; percentage of women with limited access to abortion and/or contraception; funding cuts to U.S. family planning clinics; Bulgarian ruling on the Istanbul Convention; statistics on sexual assault and E.U. nations' failure to recognize non-consensual sex as rape; plight of disabled women in Somalia; relative murder rates of Indigenous women in Canada; attacks on feminists and LGBTQ activists by anti-rights groups: Amnesty International, "Rights Today 2018," 4–5.

On percentages of women in parliamentary and head-of-state/government positions: "Women in Politics: 2019" (interactive map), Inter-Parliamentary Union, https://www.ipu.org/resources/publications/infographics/2019-03/women-in-politics-2019.

CHAPTER TWO: THE MATING GAME

On Arcangela Tarabotti: Stephen Greenblatt, *The Rise and Fall of Adam and Eve* (New York: W.W. Norton, 2017), 134–36; Arcangela Tarabotti, *Paternal Tyranny*, ed. and trans. Letizia Panizza (1654; reprint, Chicago: University of Chicago Press, 2004).

Wollstonecraft's views on reason vs. feelings: Mary Wollstonecraft, *A Vindication of the Rights of Women* (1792; reprint, London: Oxford University Press, 2009); *Stanford Encyclopedia of Philosophy*, s.v. "Mary Wollstonecraft," section 2, "Pedagogical Writings," https://plato.stanford.edu/entries/wollstonecraft/.

On non-monogamous prehistoric sexual partnerships: Christopher Ryan and Cacilda Jethá, *Sex at Dawn: The Prehistoric Origins of Modern Sexuality* (New York: HarperCollins, 2010); Christopher Ryan, interview on *Equal Time for Freethought*, WBAI, December 2010, transcript published on TheHumanist.com, February 27, 2011, https://thehumanist.com/magazine/march-april-2011/features/speaking-of-sex.

On Kit Opie's assertion that monogamy is waning: Meera Senthilingam, "Why Did We Become Monogamous?," CNN, May 18, 2016, https://www.cnn.com/2016/05/17/health/sti-infanticide-human-monogamy/index.html.

On breast reduction of statues: Interview with Doris Couture-Rigert, March 13, 2019.

On gender bias in data collection, medical diagnoses, design, etc.: Caroline Criado Perez, *Invisible Women: Data Bias in a World Designed for Men* (New York: Harry N. Abrams, 2019).

On the research focus on erectile dysfunction vs. premenstrual syndrome: "There's a Gender Gap in Medical Data, and It's Costing Women Their Lives, Says This Author," *The Current*, CBC, March 11, 2019, https://www.cbc.ca/radio/thecurrent/the-current-for-march-11-2019-1.5049277/there-s-a-gender-gap-in-medical-data-and-it-s-costing-women-their-lives-says-this-author-1.5049286; Michelle Kuepper, "Why Do We Still Not Know What Causes PMS?," ResearchGate, August 12, 2016, https://www.researchgate.net/blog/post/why-do-we-still-not-know-what-causes-pms.

Alzheimer's statistics for women vs. men: Lauran Neergaard, "Why Are the Majority of Alzheimer's Patients Women?," *Globe and Mail*, July 1, 2015, updated May 15, 2018, https://www.theglobeandmail.com/life/health-and-fitness/health/why-are-the-majority-of-alzheimers-patients-women/article25218935/.

On *The World According to Garp* and its ongoing relevance: "John Irving on Why *The World According to Garp* Is More Relevant Now than He Ever Imagined," *Q*, CBC, November 12, 2018, https://www.cbc.ca/radio/q/monday-november-12-2018-john-irving-lennon-stella-and-more-1.4899439/john-irving-on-why-the-world-according-to-garp-is-more-relevant-now-than-he-ever-imagined-1.4899452; Interview with John Irving, January 2019.

On *The Cider House Rules*: Interview with John Irving, January 2019.

Dialogue from *The Cider House Rules*: John Irving, *The Cider House Rules* (New York: William Morrow, 1985), 488.

On John Stuart Mills's view of the consequences of objectifying women: *Stanford Encyclopedia*, s.v. "John Stuart Mill," 4.4.

On Pat Barker's *The Silence of the Girls*: Emily Wilson, "A Feminist *Iliad*," review of *The Silence of the Girls*, by Pat Barker, *The Guardian*, August 22, 2018, https://www.theguardian.com/books/2018/aug/22/silence-of-the-girls-pat-barker-book-review-iliad; Pat Barker, *The Silence of the Girls* (London: Hamish Hamilton, 2018), particularly 16, 156, 267, 297.

On Eva Penavic: Sally Armstrong, "Eva: Witness for Women," *Homemaker's*, summer 1993.

On the Taliban rule in Afghanistan: Armstrong, *Veiled Threat*, 66.

Beshra and Badia's story: Sally Armstrong, "Yazidi Women Tell Their Horrific Stories," *Maclean's*, August 30, 2016, https://www.macleans.ca/news/yazidi-women-tell-their-horrific-stories/; Sally Armstrong, "'I Want My Voice to Be Heard': How Two Yazidi Sisters Escaped ISIS Captors," *The Current*, CBC, May 23, 2017, https://www.cbc.ca/radio/thecurrent/the-current-for-may-23-2017-1.4126732/i-want-my-voice-to-be-heard-how-two-yazidi-sisters-escaped-isis-captors-1.4126753; Sally Armstrong, "After ISIS Attacks, Yazidi Survivors Fight for Their Way of Life," *United Christian Observer*, June 1, 2017, https://

broadview.org/after-isis-attacks-yazidi-survivors-fight-for-their-ancient-way-of-life/.

On interviewing isis fighters in Duhok: "isis Fighters Speak to Sally Armstrong," ctv, December 24, 2017, https://www.ctvnews.ca/video?clipId=996586; Sally Armstrong, "The Real Faces of isis," *Maclean's*, August 11, 2016, https://www.macleans.ca/news/world/the-real-faces-of-isis-sally-armstrong-reports-from-iraq/.

On the Jian Ghomeshi affair and its fallout: Sally Armstrong, "Jian Ghomeshi Scandal Has Prompted Important Conversation about Sexual Assault," *Toronto Star*, November 5, 2014, https://www.thestar.com/opinion/commentary/2014/11/05/jian_ghomeshi_scandal_has_prompted_important_conversation_about_sexual_assault.html.

On campus date rape and Jameis Winston: *The Hunting Ground*, directed by Kirby Dick (Los Angeles: Chain Camera Pictures, 2015); Ken Belson, "Buccaneers' Jameis Winston Suspended for 3 Games," *New York Times*, June 28, 2018, https://www.nytimes.com/2018/06/28/sports/football/buccaneers-jameis-winston-suspended.html.

On Young Women for Change in Afghanistan: Armstrong, *Ascent of Women*, 17; and Sally Armstrong, "The New Revolutionaries," *Ideas*, cbc Radio, October 3, 4, 2011.

On the Nazra Center for Feminist Studies: Armstrong, *Ascent of Women*, 224–25.

On the YouTube child bride social experiment: Coby Persin, "65 Year Old Man Marries 12 Year Old Girl! (Child Marriage Social Experiment)," February 21, 2016, https://www.youtube.com/watch?v=KldFGgUTqKA.

Statistics on child marriage in the U.S.: Anjali Tsui, Dan Nolan, and Chris Amico, "Child Marriage in America: By the Numbers," *Frontline*, pbs, July 6, 2017, http://apps.frontline.org/child-marriage-by-the-numbers/#home; "Child Marriage — Shocking Statistics," Unchained At Last, http://www.unchainedatlast.org/child-marriage-shocking-statistics/; Sarah Ferguson, "What You Need to Know about Child Marriage in the U.S.," unicef usa, October 29, 2018, https://www.unicefusa.org/stories/what-you-need-know-about-child-marriage-us/35059; Amanda Parker, "Worse than Weinstein Is the Exploitation of Florida Girls," *Sun-Sentinel* (South Florida), October 24,

2017, https://www.sun-sentinel.com/opinion/commentary/fl-op-viewpoint-florida-child-marriage-20171024-story.html.

Farida Shaheed on "culture" as a justification for oppression: Armstrong, *Ascent of Women*, 87–88.

Statistics on child marriage worldwide: "Child Marriage Atlas," Girls Not Brides, https://www.girlsnotbrides.org/where-does-it-happen/atlas/#/.

On marriage laws in Afghanistan vs. Florida: Heather Barr, "Afghanistan Has a Tougher Law on Child Marriage than Florida," iNews, October 19, 2017, https://inews.co.uk/opinion/comment/afghanistan-florida-common-serious-child-marriage-problem/.

On judges in Nuremberg who didn't want women crying in the courtroom: Armstrong, *Ascent of Women*, 48–49.

On sexuality in sports marketing: Sally Armstrong, "Olympia's Secret," *Chatelaine*, September 2000; Caroline Wilson, "A Naked Desire to Win Some Credibility," *Sydney Morning Herald*, September 11, 2000.

On Vancouver MP Margaret Mitchell on domestic violence in the House of Commons in 1982: Judy Stoffman, "MP Margaret Mitchell Famously Called Wife Abuse 'No Laughing Matter,'" *Globe and Mail*, March 22, 2017, updated May 17, 2018, https://www.theglobeandmail.com/news/politics/mp-margaret-mitchell-famously-called-wife-abuse-no-laughing-matter/article34392492/.

On the shortage of brides for eighty million men in China and India: Heather Barr, "You Should Be Worrying about the Woman Shortage," Human Rights Watch, December 4, 2018, https://www.hrw.org/news/2018/12/04/you-should-be-worrying-about-woman-shortage.

CHAPTER THREE: A HOLY PARADOX

On the nun with blue teeth: A. Radini, M. Tromp, et. al., "Medieval Women's Early Involvement in Manuscript Production Suggested by Lapis Lazuli Identification in Dental Calculus," *Science Advances* 5, no.

1 (January 9, 2019), https://advances.sciencemag.org/content/5/1/eaau7126; "Illuminating Women's Role in the Creation of Medieval Manuscripts," Max Planck Institute for the Science of Human History, January 9, 2019, https://www.shh.mpg.de/1162492/lapis-warinner; Email interview with Christina Warinner, February 2019.

On Hildegard von Bingen: Charles Moffat, "Hildegard von Bingen: The Biography of a Feminist Nun," *The Feminist eZine*, 2002, http://www.feministezine.com/feminist/HildegardVonBingen-FeministNun.html; *Hildegard of Bingen's Unknown Language: An Edition, Translation, and Discussion*, ed. and trans. Sarah Higley (Basingstoke, UK: Palgrave Macmillan, 2007).

Aristotle on women's nature: Quoted in Simone de Beauvoir, *The Second Sex* (New York: Vintage, 2011), 5.

St. Augustine on women: Valerie Tarico, "Christian Leaders Have Always Been Misogynists," Salon.com, July 2, 2013, https://www.salon.com/2013/07/02/christians_have_always_been_misogynists_partner/.

Passage from the rabbinical gloss to the Talmud (Sanhedrin 71a:8): https://www.sefaria.org/Sanhedrin.70b.17?lang=bi&with=all&lang2=en.

On Pat Robertson's letter to the Christian Coalition: Associated Press, "Robertson Letter Attacks Feminists," *New York Times*, August 26, 1992, https://www.nytimes.com/1992/08/26/us/robertson-letter-attacks-feminists.html.

As of July 2019, thirty-two U.S. states have made FGM illegal, and since 1996, federal legislation has protected girls under the age of eighteen: "U.S. Laws Against FGM — State by State," Equality Now, https://www.equalitynow.org/us_laws_against_fgm_state_by_state.

On the 160 Kenyan girls who sued their government: Sally Armstrong, "Kenyan Girls' Quest for Justice Realized, with Canadian Help," *Toronto Star*, March 12, 2017, https://www.thestar.com/news/insight/2017/03/12/kenyan-girls-quest-for-justice-realized-with-canadian-help.html.

On U.S. federal and state laws banning FGM: Equality Now, "US Laws Against FGM"; "FGM in the US," Equality Now, https://www.equalitynow.org/FGM_in_the_us_learn_more.

Global statistics on FGM: "Female Genital Mutilation: Key Facts," World Health Organization; Rebecca Ratcliffe, "FGM Rates in East Africa Drop from 71% to 8% in 20 Years, Study Shows," *The Guardian*, November 7, 2018, https://www.theguardian.com/global-development/2018/nov/07/FGM-rates-in-east-africa-drop-20-years-study-shows.

On Molly Melching, the village of Malicounda Bambara in Senegal, and FGM: Armstrong, *Ascent of Women*, 108–12.

On foot binding and infanticide of daughters: Armstrong, *Veiled Threat*, 85, 94, 100, 101; Gerry Mackie, "Ending Footbinding and Infibulation: A Convention Account," *American Sociological Review* 61 (December 1996) 1001, https://pages.ucsd.edu/~gmackie/documents/MackieASR.pdf.

On honour killings: Sally Armstrong, "Honour's Victims," *Chatelaine*, March 2000.

On Jordanian law vis-à-vis honour killings: *Encyclopaedia Britannica Online*, s.v. "Honor Killing," https://www.britannica.com/topic/honor-killing.

On Jalal Aljabri and honour killings: Armstrong, "Honour's Victims."

On Ramallah doctors, the obsession with female purity, and emancipation through political power: Armstrong, *Veiled Threat*, 103.

On the Absher app in Saudi Arabia: Mathew Ingram, "Google, Apple, and the Saudi Wife-Tracking App," *Columbia Journalism Review*, March 11, 2019, https://www.cjr.org/analysis/google-saudi-wife-tracking-app.php.

On Saudi Arabia's Global Gender Gap Index ranking: *The Global Gender Gap Report 2018* (Geneva: World Economic Forum, 2018), 11, https://www.weforum.org/reports/the-global-gender-gap-report-2018.

On Saudi Arabia's "eye for an eye" justice: Rob Williams, "Saudi Arabia Court Orders Man to Be Surgically Paralysed in 'Eye for an Eye' Punishment, *The Independent*, April 4, 2013, https://www.independent.co.uk/news/world/middle-east/saudi-arabian-court-orders-man-to-be-surgically-paralysed-in-eye-for-an-eye-punishment-8559869.

html; "Saudi Arabia: Free Detainee in 'Eye-for-an-Eye' Case," Human Rights Watch, April 13, 2013, https://www.hrw.org/news/2013/04/13/saudi-arabia-free-detainee-eye-eye-case.

On Saudi Arabia's guardianship system: "Saudi Arabia: 10 Reasons Why Women Flee," Human Rights Watch, January 30, 2019, https://www.hrw.org/news/2019/01/30/saudi-arabia-10-reasons-why-women-flee.

On the honour killing in Kingston: Michael Friscolanti, "Inside the Shafia Killings That Shocked a Nation," *Maclean's*, March 3, 2016, https://www.macleans.ca/news/canada/inside-the-shafia-killings-that-shocked-a-nation/.

On Debbie Palmer and polygamy in the FLDS: Armstrong: *Ascent of Women*, 70–85.

On breast ironing: Stan Ziv, "Showing Love Through Breast Ironing: Why Some Daughters Endure This Painful Practice to Appease Their Mothers," *Newsweek*, August 3, 2017, https://www.newsweek.com/2017/08/11/breast-ironing-painful-girls-going-through-puberty-cameroon-mothers-often-do-645388.html.

Statistics and legislation on child marriage in Malawi: "Malawi," Girls Not Brides, https://www.girlsnotbrides.org/child-marriage/malawi/; "Malawi Parliament Adopts Amendment to End Child Marriage," UN Women, February 22, 2017, http://www.unwomen.org/en/news/stories/2017/2/news-malawi-parliament-adopts-amendment-to-end-child-marriage.

On Chief Mwanza's campaign: Henry Chimbali, "When Women Rule: Malawi Chief Battles Harms Against Girls," United Nations Population Fund, January 24, 2019, https://www.unfpa.org/news/when-women-rule-malawi-chief-battles-harms-against-girls.

On Chief Kachindamoto's campaign: Hannah McNeish, "Malawi's Fearsome Chief, Terminator of Child Marriages," Al Jazeera, May 19, 2016, https://www.aljazeera.com/indepth/features/2016/03/malawi-fearsome-chief-terminator-child-marriages-160316081809603.html.

On the Bishop Mulakkal case: Maria Abi-Habib and Suhasini Raj, "Nun's Rape Case Against Bishop Shakes a Catholic Bastion in India," *New York Times*, February 9, 2019, https://www.nytimes.com/2019/02/09/world/asia/nun-rape-india-bishop.html; "Kerala Nun Rape Case: SIT

Files Charge Sheet Against Bishop Mulakkal, Names 83 Witnesses," Mirror Now Digital, April 9, 2019, https://www.timesnownews.com/mirror-now/in-focus/article/kerala-nun-rape-case-bishop-jalandhar-franco-mulakkal-sit-chargesheet-sos-pala-fcc-nuns-protest/397169; Swati Gupta and Subhrangshu Pratim Sarmah, "Nuns Who Protested Indian Bishop Accused of Rape Say Church Trying to Silence Them," CNN, January 29, 2019, https://www.cnn.com/2019/01/29/asia/india-nuns-kerala-intl/index.html.

On the Pennsylvania grand jury report: Laurie Goodstein and Sharon Otterman, "Catholic Priests Abused 1,000 Children in Pennsylvania, Report Says," *New York Times*, August 14, 2018, https://www.nytimes.com/2018/08/14/us/catholic-church-sex-abuse-pennsylvania.html.

On the post-2014 circumstances of Afghan women and President Trump's peace-talk overtures to the Taliban: Sally Armstrong, "Afghanistan's Women Will Not Be Victims of Peace," *Globe and Mail*, February 15, 2019, https://www.theglobeandmail.com/opinion/article-afghanistans-women-will-not-be-victims-of-peace/.

On Afghanistan: From my many assignments in Afghanistan during the Taliban regime between 1997 and 2018.

Farida Shaheed on religion and women: Armstrong, *Ascent of Women*, 67.

On the lot of women in 1000 CE: Lyn Reese, "Women in the Year 1000 CE," Women in World History Curriculum, http://www.womeninworldhistory.com/women1000.html.

On the Istanbul Convention: Maya Oppenheim, "Austerity Cuts Blamed for UK Failure to Ratify Pan-European Convention Combatting Violence Against Women," *The Independent*, February 18, 2019, https://www.independent.co.uk/news/uk/home-news/uk-ratify-istanbul-convention-women-girls-rights-european-a8768606.html.

On the history of marriage and the "transactional relationship": Molly Rosen Guy, "Whatever Happened to Marrying for Love?," *Cosmopolitan Middle East*, December 27, 2018, https://www.cosmopolitanme.com/content/19014-marrying-wedding-love-advice; Stephanie Coontz, *Marriage, A History: How Love Conquered Marriage* (New York: Penguin, 2006).

On labiaplasty and vaginal rejuvenation: Janice Boddy, "The Normal and the Aberrant in Female Genital Cutting: Shifting Paradigms," *HAU, Journal of Ethnographic Theory* 6, no. 222 (2016): 41–69 (particularly 43), https://www.journals.uchicago.edu/doi/pdfplus/10.14318/hau6.2.008; Interview with Janice Boddy, October 23, 2018 and May 8, 2019.

On Sarah Grimké: *Internet Encyclopedia of Philosophy*, s.v. "Sarah Grimké (1792–1873) and Angelina Grimké Weld (1805–1879)," https://www.iep.utm.edu/grimke/; *The Public Years of Sarah and Angelina Grimké: Selected Writings 1835–1839*, ed. Larry Ceplair (New York: Columbia University Press, 1989), 208; Louise W. Knight, "The 19th-Century Powerhouse Who Inspired RBG," *CNN*, September 1, 2018, https://www.cnn.com/2018/09/01/opinions/ruth-bader-ginsburg-rbg-and-grimke-sisters-louise-knight/index.html.

CHAPTER FOUR: WHEN THE PATRIARCHY

MEETS THE MATRIARCHY

On Carolyn Bennett's remarks about Jean Chrétien's cabinet selections: Campbell Clark, "PM Scolds Liberal Dissenter," January 28, 2002, *Globe and Mail*, https://www.theglobeandmail.com/news/national/pm-scolds-liberal-dissenter/article25290684/.

Interview with Carolyn Bennett on March 30, 2019.

António Guterres on the shifting world order: Address to the General Assembly, September 25, 2018, https://www.un.org/sg/en/content/sg/speeches/2018-09-25/address-73rd-general-assembly.

On the role of social media in populism: Jamie Bartlett, "Why Is Populism Booming? Today's Tech Is Partly to Blame," *The Guardian*, November 29, 2018, https://www.theguardian.com/commentisfree/2018/nov/29/populism-tinder-politics-swipe-left-or-right-unthinkingly; Jamie Bartlett, "From Hope to Hate: How the Early Internet Fed the Far Right," *The Guardian*, August 31, 2017, https://www.theguardian.com/world/2017/aug/31/far-right-alt-right-white-supremacists-rise-online.

Number of Women's March participants worldwide: Erica Chenoweth and Jeremy Pressman, "This Is What We Learned by Counting the Women's Marches," *Washington Post*, February 27, 2017, https://www.washingtonpost.com/news/monkey-cage/wp/2017/02/07/this-is-what-we-learned-by-counting-the-womens-marches/?utm_term=.21610f4f8333.

On anti-intellectualism in American culture: Isaac Asimov, "A Cult of Ignorance," *Newsweek*, January 21, 1980, https://media.aphelis.net/wp-content/uploads/2012/04/ASIMOV_1980_Cult_of_Ignorance.pdf.

On populism's danger to the human rights movement: Kenneth Roth, "The Dangerous Rise of Populism: Global Attacks on Human Rights Values," in Human Rights Watch, *World Report 2017* (New York: Seven Stories Press, 2017), 1.

Jair Bolsonaro quote: Eliane Brum, "How a Homophobic, Misogynist, Racist 'Thing' Could Be Brazil's Next President," *The Guardian*, October 6, 2018, https://www.theguardian.com/commentisfree/2018/oct/06/homophobic-mismogynist-racist-brazil-jair-bolsonaro.

Rodrigo Duterte quote: Hannah Ellis-Petersen, "Philippines: Rodrigo Duterte Orders Soldiers to Shoot Female Rebels 'in the Vagina,'" *The Guardian*, February 13, 2018, https://www.theguardian.com/world/2018/feb/13/philippines-rodrigo-duterte-orders-soldiers-to-shoot-female-rebels-in-the-vagina.

On sexism in authoritarian politics and Peter Beinart and Valerie Hudson quotes: Peter Beinart, "The New Authoritarians Are Waging War on Women," *The Atlantic*, January/February 2019, https://www.theatlantic.com/magazine/archive/2019/01/authoritarian-sexism-trump-duterte/576382/.

On Poland's attacks on women's and LGBTQ rights: "Polish Government Campaign Encourages Citizens to 'Breed Like Rabbits,'" Euronews, November 9, 2017, https://www.euronews.com/2017/11/09/polish-government-campaign-encourages-citizens-to-breed-like-rabbits; "'The Breath of the Government on My Back': Attacks on Women's Rights in Poland," Human Rights Watch, February 6, 2019, https://www.hrw.org/sites/default/files/report_pdf/poland0219_web2_0.pdf.

On Italy's attacks on women's and LGBTQ rights: Kara Fox and Valentina Di Donato, "Abortion Is a Right in Italy. For Many Women, Getting One Is Nearly Impossible," CNN, https://edition.cnn.com/interactive/2019/05/europe/italy-abortion-intl/.

On Viktor Orbán: Shaun Walker, "Viktor Orbán: No Tax for Hungarian Women with Four or More Children," *The Guardian*, February 10, 2019, https://www.theguardian.com/world/2019/feb/10/viktor-orban-no-tax-for-hungarian-women-with-four-or-more-children; Shaun Walker, "'We Won't Keep Quiet Again': The Women Taking on Viktor Orbán," *The Guardian*, December 21, 2018, https://www.theguardian.com/world/2018/dec/21/hungary-female-politicians-viktor-orban.

On women's protests in Italy: Jane Fae, "As Italy Indulges a Nationalist Agenda, Women's Rights Are Being Steadily Eroded," *The Independent*, December 22, 2018, https://www.independent.co.uk/news/long_reads/italy-womens-rights-abortion-gender-equality-feminism-lega-politics-a8690541.html.

On #TimesUp: "700,000 Female Farmworkers Say They Stand with Hollywood Actors Against Sexual Assault," *Time*, November 10, 2017, https://time.com/5018813/farmworkers-solidarity-hollywood-sexual-assault/.

On Mike Pence's dining policy: Alana Vagianos, "Kamala Harris Says It's 'Outrageous' That Mike Pence Won't Meet Alone with Women," *Huffington Post*, March 15, 2019, https://www.huffingtonpost.ca/entry/kamala-harris-mike-pence-women_n_5c8bcae8e4b03e83bdc06674.

On Zuzana Čaputová: Sheena McKenzie, "Slovakia's 'Erin Brockovich' Elected First Female President, in Rebuke of Populism," CNN, March 31, 2019, https://www.cnn.com/2019/03/31/europe/slovakia-elects-president-zuzana-caputova-intl/index.html.

On donations to Planned Parenthood after the 2016 U.S. election: Katie Mettler, "People Are Donating to Planned Parenthood in Mike Pence's Name," *Washington Post*, November 15, 2016, https://www.washingtonpost.com/news/morning-mix/wp/2016/11/15/people-are-donating-to-planned-parenthood-in-mike-pences-name/?utm_term=.a0da3cae8263; Erica Gonzales, "Mila Kunis Donates to Planned Parenthood under Mike Pence's Name Every Month," *Harper's Bazaar*,

November 6, 2017, https://www.harpersbazaar.com/celebrity/latest/a13438965/mila-kunis-planned-parenthood-mike-pence/; "Planned Parenthood Has Already Received 82,000 Donations from 'Mike Pence,'" *The Cut*, December 8, 2016, https://www.thecut.com/2016/12/how-many-planned-parenthood-donations-came-from-mike-pence.html.

On the lawsuit against the government of Alabama: Zoe Tillman, "The ACLU and Planned Parenthood Are Suing Alabama over the State's New Abortion Law," BuzzFeed News, May 24, 2019, https://www.buzzfeednews.com/article/zoetillman/aclu-planned-parenthood-suing-alabama-abortion-law.

On masculinity in the MENA region: Shereen El Feki, Brian Heilman, and Gary Barker, eds., *Understanding Masculinities: Results from the International Men and Gender Equality Survey (IMAGES) — Middle East and North Africa* (Cairo and Washington, DC: UN Women and Promundo-US, 2017), particularly 2, 14–16, 263, https://promundoglobal.org/wp-content/uploads/2017/05/IMAGES-MENA-Multi-Country-Report-EN-16May2017-web.pdf.

On Steve Bannon's fear of #MeToo: Joshua Green, *Devil's Bargain: Steve Bannon, Donald Trump, and the Nationalist Uprising*, 2nd ed. (New York: Penguin, 2018), xxiii, xxiv; Eliza Relman, "Steve Bannon Warns That Women Are Going to 'Take Charge of Society,'" *Business Insider*, February 12, 2018, https://www.businessinsider.com/steve-bannon-oprah-women-take-charge-of-society-2018-2.

On Hillary Clinton's 1995 speech in Beijing: "Hillary Clinton Declares 'Women's Rights Are Human Rights,'" *Washington Week*, PBS, September 8, 1995, https://www.pbs.org/weta/washingtonweek/web-video/hillary-clinton-declares-womens-rights-are-human-rights; Gayle Tzemach Lemmon, "The Hillary Doctrine," *Newsweek*, March 6, 2011, https://www.newsweek.com/hillary-doctrine-66l0.

Phumzile Mlambo-Ngcuka on the growing number of women ministers: "Proportion of Women Ministers All-Time High, IPU/UN Women Map Shows," XinhuaNet, March 13, 2019, http://www.xinhuanet.com/english/2019-03/13/c_137889777.htm.

On the 30 percent threshold and critical mass theory: R. M. Kanter, "Some Effects of Proportions on Group Life: Skewed Sex Roles and

Responses to Token Women," *American Journal of Sociology* 82, no. 5 (1977): 965–90; Sarah Childs and Mona Lena Krook, "Critical Mass Theory and Women's Political Representation," *Political Studies* 56. no. 3 (2008): 725–36.

Statistics on representation of women in national parliaments: Inter-Parliamentary Union, "Women in National Parliaments," updated February 1, 2019, http://archive.ipu.org/wmn-e/classif.htm.

Sylvia Bashevkin on the 30 percent critical mass theory: Interview with Sylvia Bashevkin, April 3, 2019.

On the IPU/UN findings on women in ministerial positions: "One in Five Ministers Is a Woman, According to New IPU/UN Women Map," UN Women, March 12, 2019, http://www.unwomen.org/en/news/stories/2019/3/press-release--ipu-un-women-map-women-in-politics.

On proposed new areas of focus in critical mass theory: Sarah Childs and Mona Lena Krook, "Gender and Politics: The State of the Art," *Politics* 26, no.1 (2006): 18–28.

On the Canadian government's 2019 parental leave option for second parents: Ivona Hideg, "New Parental-Leave Benefit Inches Us Ever Closer Toward Gender Equality," *Globe and Mail*, March 29, 2019, https://www.theglobeandmail.com/opinion/article-new-parental-leave-benefit-inches-us-ever-closer-toward-gender/.

On the benefits of paternity leave: Eric Arthrell, "Why Longer Paternity Leave Is Big Win for Women," *American Banker*, October 10, 2017, https://www.americanbanker.com/opinion/longer-paternity-leave-correlates-with-a-big-win-for-women; *The Design of Everyday Men: A New Lens for Gender Equality Progress*, Deloitte, 2019, https://www2.deloitte.com/content/dam/insights/us/articles/ca1671_design-of-everyday-men/DI_The-design-of-everyday-men.pdf.

On the 30% Club: "Who We Are," 30% Club, https://30percentclub.org/about/who-we-are; "US 30% Club," Boyden, https://www.boyden.com/united-states/us-30-club/index.html; "Women on Board," 30% Club U.S., https://us.30percentclub.org/initiative/women-on-board/; "TSX Composite Index — 23.9%," 30% Club Canada, https://30percentclub.org/about/chapters/canada.

Spencer Lanthier on progress of gender representation in business: Interview with Spencer Lanthier, April 3 and April 7, 2019.

Sweden's 3R feminist foreign policy: Rachel Vogelstein and Alexandra Bro, "Sweden's Feminist Foreign Policy, Long May It Reign," *Financial Post*, January 30, 2019, https://foreignpolicy.com/2019/01/30/sweden-feminist-foreignpolicy/; James Rupert, "Sweden's Foreign Minister Explains Feminist Foreign Policy," United States Institute of Peace, February 9, 2015, https://www.usip.org/publications/2015/02/swedens-foreign-minister-explains-feminist-foreign-policy; Jenny Nordberg, "Who's Afraid of a Feminist Foreign Policy?," *New Yorker*, April 15, 2015, https://www.newyorker.com/news/news-desk/swedens-feminist-foreign-minister.

On the effectiveness of peace processes when women take part: "Women's Participation in Peace Processes," Council on Foreign Relations, updated January 30, 2019, https://www.cfr.org/interactive/womens-participation-in-peace-processes.

On the potential impact on global GDP of eliminating the workforce gender gap: Vogelstein and Bro, "Sweden's Feminist Foreign Policy."

Global Affairs Canada on the feminist international assistance policy: "Plan at a Glance and Operating Context," Global Affairs Canada, https://www.international.gc.ca/gac-amc/priorities-priorites.aspx?lang=eng.

On the "global gag rule" imposed by Donald Trump: "Global Gag Rule," Center for Health and Gender Equity, updated July 2018, http://www.genderhealth.org/files/uploads/change/publications/CHANGE_GGR_Policy_Brief.pdf.

On Canadian announcements of funding for women's health and rights: Amanda Connolly, "Trudeau Pledges $300m to Boost Sexual, Reproductive Health Aid by 2023," Global News, June 4, 2019, https://globalnews.ca/news/5350798/liberals-reproductive-rights-funding/; Tara Patricia Cookson and Lorena Fuentes, "For Equality, Women Need Power in Their Hands," *Toronto Star*, June 11, 2019, https://www.thestar.com/opinion/contributors/2019/06/11/for-women-need-to-reach-equality-is-power-in-their-hands.html.

OpenCanada roundtable of international women leaders: "10 Reasons Why We Need Feminist Foreign Policy," OpenCanada.

org / Centre for International Governance Innovation, March 7, 2018, https://www.opencanada.org/features/10-reasons-why-we-need-feminist-foreign-policy/.

On the Indian Act: "Marginalization of Indigenous Women," Indigenous Foundations, University of British Columbia, https://indigenousfoundations.arts.ubc.ca/marginalization_of_aboriginal_women/; Mary Eberts, "'A High Risk Lifestyle': Being an Indigenous Woman," in *Making Space for Indigenous Feminism*, ed. Joyce Green, 2nd ed. (Halifax and Winnipeg: Fernwood, 2017), 145; Wayne Brown, "Mary Two-Axe Earley: Crusader for Equal Rights for Aboriginal Women," *Electoral Insight*, Elections Canada, November 2003, https://www.elections.ca/content.aspx?section=res&dir=eim/issue9&document=p10&lang=e.

On the National Inquiry into Missing and Murdered Indigenous Women and Girls: Gloria Galloway, "Inquiry Finds 'Race-Based Genocide' of Indigenous People in Canada," *Globe and Mail*, June 3, 2019; John Paul Tasker, "Confusion Reigns over Number of Missing, Murdered Indigenous Women," CBC, February 16, 2016, updated February 17, 2016, https://www.cbc.ca/news/politics/mmiw-4000-hajdu-1.3450237.

On intersectionality: "What Does Intersectional Feminism Actually Mean?," International Women's Development Agency, May 11, 2018, www.iwda.org.au/what-does-intersectional-feminism-actually-mean.

On the 160 Kenyan girls who sued their government: Armstrong, "Kenyan Girls."

On the kidnapping of the Chibok girls: Sally Armstrong, "Women as Weapons of War," *Ottawa Citizen*, October 24, 2014, https://ottawacitizen.com/news/politics/women-as-weapons-of-war.

CHAPTER FIVE: SHIFTING POWER

Tucker Carlson quote: "Tucker Carlson Says Women Making More Money than Men Leads to 'More Drug and Alcohol Abuse, Higher Incarceration Rates,'" Media Matters, January 2, 2019, https://

www.mediamatters.org/video/2019/01/02/tucker-carlson-says-women-making-more-money-men-leads-more-drug-and-alcohol-abuse-higher/222400.

Ben Bernanke on women in the field of economics: Ben Casselman and Jim Tankersley, "Female Economists Push Their Field Toward a #MeToo Reckoning," *New York Times*, January 10, 2019, https://www.nytimes.com/2019/01/10/business/economics-sexual-harassment-metoo.html.

On gender pay gaps across professions and demographics in the U.S.: Lydia Dishman, "This Is the Impact of the Gender Wage Gap," *Fast Company*, April 10, 2018, https://www.fastcompany.com/40556360/this-is-the-impact-of-gender-wage-gap; and "These Jobs Have the Largest and Smallest Gender Pay Gaps," *Fast Company*, September 27, 2017, https://www.fastcompany.com/40474000/these-jobs-have-the-largest-and-smallest-gender-pay-gaps.

On gender pay gaps in the U.K.: "Four Big Lessons from the UK's New Gender Pay Gap Reporting Rules and What's Next for Equality," *The Conversation*, August 16, 2018, https://theconversation.com/four-big-lessons-from-the-uks-new-gender-pay-gap-reporting-rules-and-whats-next-for-equality-100924.

On the economic consequences of sidelining women: "Helping Ensure Growth Is Shared by Men and Women," World Bank, October 1, 2018, https://www.worldbank.org/en/topic/gender/brief/helping-ensure-growth-is-shared-by-men-and-women; "Why India Needs Women to Work," *The Economist*, July 5, 2018, https://www.economist.com/leaders/2018/07/05/why-india-needs-women-to-work; "Closing the Crop Gap: Empowering Women to Feed the World," Pepsico, February 19, 2019, www.pepsico.com/news/stories/closing-the-crop-gap-empowering-women-to-feed-the-world.

On Gowramma's initiative: Armstrong, *Ascent of Women*, 161–65.

On Grameen Bank: Armstrong, *Ascent of Women*, 155–58.

Michael Cole-Fontayn quote: "BNY Mellon and United Nations Foundation Reveal Investment Opportunities for Closing the Global Gender Gap in 'Return on Equality,'" United Nations Foundation, January 19, 2017, https://unfoundation.org/media/

bny-mellon-and-united-nations-foundation-reveal-investment-opportunities-for-closing-the-global-gender-gap-in-return-on-equality/.

Quotes from *Moment of Lift*: Melinda Gates, *The Moment of Lift: How Empowering Women Changes the World* (New York: Flatiron Books, 2019), 211–12, 234.

Dona Eull-Schultz on exerting financial leverage: Interview with Dona Eull-Schultz, April 12, 2019.

Comment from Camilla Sutton, and stats on women in capital markets: Interview with Camilla Sutton, December 17, 2018.

On the dearth of women in the Canadian tech sector: Ayman Antoun, "On Skills and Gender, Canadian Business Can No Longer Just Mind the Gap," *Globe and Mail*, March 7, 2019, https://www.theglobeandmail.com/business/careers/leadership/article-ibm-canada-the-time-is-now-for-businesses-to-address-the-skills/.

On the cost of undereducating girls and the slow progress of gender pay gap change: Nikki van der Gaag, *Feminism and Men* (London: Zed Books, 2014), 115–16.

On the 2019 appointment of women to head all five UN economic sectors: "A World First: Women at the Helm of Every UN Commission," *UN News*, April 27, 2019, https://news.un.org/en/story/2019/04/1037171.

On the Geena Davis Institute: Armstrong, *Ascent of Women* (Toronto: Vintage Canada, 2014), 229–31.

Blind spots and gender expectations at school and work: (Delee Fromm, *Understanding Gender at Work: How to Use, Lose and Expose Blind Spots for Career Success*, (Victoria, BC: Tellwell Talent, 2017), 90, 162, 193.

On women disguising themselves as men: Meghan Demaria, "11 Badass Women in History Who Pretended to Be Men Because Gender Equality Back Then Was More Myth than Reality," *Bustle*, September 25, 2015, https://www.bustle.com/articles/112732-11-badass-women-in-history-who-pretended-to-be-men-because-gender-equality-back-then-was.

On Agnes Macphail: Sylvia Bashevkin, *Women, Power, Politics: The Hidden Story of Canada's Unfinished Democracy* (Toronto: Oxford University Press, 2009) 60–61; Terry Crowley, *Agnes Macphail and the Politics of Equality* (Toronto: James Lorimer, 1990), 94.

On Shauna Hunt's confrontation with participants in a sexist meme: Ashley Csanady, "Hydro One Employee Fired over Sexual Harassment of a Reporter Has Been Rehired," *National Post*, November 2, 2015, https://nationalpost.com/news/politics/hydro-one-employee-fired-over-sexual-harassment-of-a-reporter-has-been-rehired.

On the online harassment survey by Troll Busters and the International Women's Media Foundation: "Trolls and Threats: Online Harassment of Female Journalists," Al Jazeera, October 6, 2018, https://www.aljazeera.com/programmes/listeningpost/2018/10/trolls-threats-online-harassment-female-journalists-181006101141463.html.

On online abuse stifling participation in social media debates: "Cyberbullying Restricts Young Women's Voices Online," European Institute of Gender Equality, October 11, 2018, https://eige.europa.eu/news/cyberbullying-restricts-young-womens-voices-online.

On online abuse inflicted on women in media: "IFJ Global Survey Shows Massive Impact of Online Abuse on Women Journalists," International Federation of Journalists, November 13, 2018, https://www.ifj.org/media-centre/news/detail/article/ifj-global-survey-shows-massive-impact-of-online-abuse-on-women-journalists.html.

On the Bethesda–Chevy Chase High School incident: Samantha Schmidt, "Teenage Boys Rated Their Female Classmates Based on Looks. The Girls Fought Back," *Washington Post*, March 26, 2019, https://www.washingtonpost.com/lifestyle/2019/03/26/teen-boys-rated-their-female-classmates-based-looks-girls-fought-back/?utm_term=.320d36b98221.

Deloitte study on men and gender roles: *The Design of Everyday Men*.

On the author's experience in Baidoa: Sally Armstrong, *Bitter Roots, Tender Shoots: The Uncertain Fate of Afghanistan's Women* (Toronto: Viking Canada, 2008), 108–9.

The internet as "amplifier of disruption": Bartlett, *Radicals*, 2.

On preconditions for ideas to enter the mainstream: Bartlett, *Radicals*, 313.

Nikki van der Gaag's discouragement of softly-softly tactics: Van der Gaag, *Feminism and Men*, 115–16.

On the Women of Liberia Mass Action for Peace: Leymah Gbowee, *Mighty Be Our Powers: How Sisterhood, Prayer, and Sex Changed a Nation at War* (New York: Beast Books, 2011), 140.

On imaging technology and the gendered brain: Louann Brizendine, *The Female Brain* (New York: Broadway Books, 2006), 4.

John Gray on interplanetary undertones of gender differences: John Gray, *Men Are from Mars, Women Are from Venus*, 20th anniversary ed. (New York: HarperCollins, 2012).

On prehistoric cave art, finger fluting, and intimacy: Leslie Van Gelder, "Cave Art and Enduring Kindness," TEDx Talk, Queenstown, New Zealand, April 19, 2015, https://www.youtube.com/watch?v=BYGPcohf5Ss.

On Yannis Bahrakis: "Pulitzer-Winning Reuters Photographer Dies Aged 58," *The Guardian*, March 3, 2019, https://www.theguardian.com/media/2019/mar/03/pulitzer-prize-winning-reuters-photographer-yannis-behrakis-dies-aged-58.

PERMISSIONS

Permission is gratefully acknowledged to reprint excerpts from the following:

(p. 33) The passage on Confucianism and the marriage system is reprinted by permission of Xiongya Gao.

(pp. 206–11) The foreign-policy comments from women around the world have been reprinted by permission of OpenCanada.org / The Centre for International Governance Innovation.

(pp. 164–65) The open letter by Sabha Sajjad-Hazai is reprinted by permission of the author.

ACKNOWLEDGEMENTS

THIS HAS BEEN THE assignment of a lifetime; I am delighted and humbled to join the list of Massey lecturers whom I have listened to and read over many decades. First among the people to thank is Paul Kennedy, the just retired host of *Ideas*. I haven't kept count of how many car rides I have taken with Paul and his program, or how many parking lots I lingered in to hear the end of another great interview, or how many snowstorms I navigated while listening to "the voice." And who can calculate the amount of information and education and entertainment this man has brought to all of us as host of *Ideas*? He's brilliant and generous too with his vast amount of knowledge. And he's been my guide and my supporter and sometimes my conscience throughout the Massey odyssey. My ever grateful thanks to you, Paul.

There is a group of people I relied on throughout the writing of the Masseys — anthropologists and archaeologists who were willing to share their valuable, sometimes incredible, and often moving research with me. In particular, April Nowell, an anthropologist and professor (and great storyteller) at the University of Victoria, B.C.; Leslie Van Gelder, an archaeologist, writer, and researcher (and world expert on finger fluting in caves) who lives in New Zealand; Christina Warinner, an anthropologist who teaches at the University of Oklahoma in the U.S. and is W2 Group Leader at the Max Planck Institute for the Science of Human History in Jena, Germany; and Doris Couture-Rigert, chief of Conservation and Technical Research at the National Gallery of Canada. Their patience with my many questions and their interest in sharing the fascinating work that they do took my research to places I had only dreamed about reaching.

Tim Draimin — social innovator, executive director of SiG (Social Innovation Generation), and senior advisor at the J. W. McConnell Family Foundation — helped me enormously with the research that predicts the rise and fall of movements such as #MeToo.

Writing the Massey Lectures means you are doing almost nothing else for a year but chasing research and interviews and hoping it all comes together before each chapter deadline. During that frantic period, your friends and family forgive you for ignoring them, all the while being forever on hand to help. My daughter Anna MacQuarrie agreed to read the first drafts of the manuscript and gave me her feedback as a human rights expert; my son Peter Armstrong and daughter Heather Armstrong provided endless research tips and Chardonnay. My sister Rhody Sadler did what big sisters always do — she cheered for me. Writer Ernest Hillen kept a welcome vigil on my deadlines with heaps of encouraging words, and financial wizard Dona Eull-Schultz walked me through the economics of inequality, a minefield if ever there was one. My friend Maggie Hayes somehow managed to scan dozens of sources and kept new data flowing to me, usually after listening to me complain about the difficulty of verifying a piece of enticing information. And for the best epigraph research, thank you to my friend Catherine Eddy. I am so grateful to all of you for steering me to the finish line.

The team at House of Anansi is remarkable. Sarah MacLachlan, president and publisher, with her publishing wisdom and we-can-do-anything attitude, set the pace. Janie Yoon, the talented associate publisher, worked tirelessly to turn my manuscript into the lectures I hoped they would be. And Peter Norman did an absolutely outstanding job with the copy edit and fact checking. Gillian Watts did the proofreading and indexing. Allegra Robinson helped with additional fact checking. The marvelous Maria Golikova was the shepherd who brought all of this together. My thanks to these professionals who labour so intensely over thoughts and anecdotes; who care so much about facts and language and grammar and above all a book with a story to tell. I learned so much at their hands and am enormously grateful for the effort they put into *Power Shift*. And to Laura Meyer, publicity director, and her fast-moving team of promotion artists — thank you.

I am forever in debt to the CBC team at *Ideas*, executive director Greg Kelly and producer Philip Coulter, smart, creative people who know the heartbeat of the Massey Lectures, whether it be the cities the lectures are in, the people who attend, or the style and content of the fifty-eight-year-old annual hit series. Working on these Massey Lectures has been enriching, exhausting, and exhilarating. Thank you for inviting me to work with you.

And to my agent Hilary McMahon, thanks for sticking with me during this extraordinary trip around the sun.

TO ACCESS THE BOOK index, please go to https://houseofanansi.com/products/power-shift.

(THE CBC MASSEY LECTURES SERIES)

All Our Relations
Tanya Talaga
978-1-4870-0573-3 (CAN)
978-1-4870-0574-0 (U.S.)

In Search of a Better World
Payam Akhavan
978-1-4870-0200-8 (CAN)
978-1-4870-0339-5 (U.S.)

Therefore Choose Life
George Wald
978-1-4870-0320-3 (CAN)
978-1-4870-0338-8 (U.S.)

The Return of History
Jennifer Welsh
978-1-4870-0242-8

History's People
Margaret MacMillan
978-1-4870-0137-7

Belonging
Adrienne Clarkson
978-1-77089-837-0 (CAN)
978-1-77089-838-7 (U.S)

Blood
Lawrence Hill
978-1-77089-322-1 (CAN)
978-1-77089-323-8 (U.S.)

The Universe Within
Neil Turok
978-1-77089-015-2 (CAN)
978-1-77089-017-6 (U.S.)

Winter
Adam Gopnik
978-0-88784-974-9 (CAN)
978-0-88784-975-6 (U.S.)

Player One
Douglas Coupland
978-0-88784-972-5 (CAN)
978-0-88784-968-8 (U.S.)

The Wayfinders
Wade Davis
978-0-88784-842-1 (CAN)
978-0-88784-766-0 (U.S.)

Payback
Margaret Atwood
978-0-88784-810-0 (CAN)
978-0-88784-800-1 (U.S.)

The City of Words
Alberto Manguel
978-0-88784-763-9

More Lost Massey Lectures
Bernie Lucht, ed.
978-0-88784-801-8

The Lost Massey Lectures
Bernie Lucht, ed.
978-0-88784-217-7

The Ethical Imagination
Margaret Somerville
978-0-88784-747-9

Race Against Time
Stephen Lewis
978-0-88784-753-0

A Short History of Progress
Ronald Wright
978-0-88784-706-6

The Truth About Stories
Thomas King
978-0-88784-696-0